Photo Credits

After I graduated from Northwestern University, I became a
lawyer and practiced law for eight years with a large firm. Then I
studied at Garrett Theological Seminary and was ordained a
United Methodist minister. I have served as pastor of three
churches. Also, I am a clinical psychologist and have worked in
mental health out-patient settings and in private practice. I have
written eighteen children's books.

Kuwait

Kuwait

BY LEILA MERRELL FOSTER

Enchantment of the World
Second Series

Children's Press®

A Division of Grolier Publishing

NEW YORK LONDON HONG KONG SYDNEY
DANBURY, CONNECTICUT

Consultant: Louay Bahry, Ph.D., Adjunct Professor of Political Science, University of Tennessee, Knoxville

Please note: All statistics are as up-to-date as possible at time of publication.

Visit Children's Press on the Internet at: http://publishing.grolier.com

Library of Congress Cataloging-in-Publication Data

Foster, Leila Merrell
        Kuwait / by Leila Merrell Foster.
        p. cm. — (Enchantment of the world. Second series)
        Includes bibliographical references (p.) and index.
Summary : Describes the history, geography, economy, language, religion, sports, arts, and people of this oil-rich country located on the northwestern shore of the Persian Gulf.
        ISBN 0-516-20604-4
        1. Kuwait—Juvenile literature. [1. Kuwait.] I. Title. II. Series.
        DS247.K82F67 1998
        915.367—dc21   97-23845
                                                               CIP
                                                               AC

To all fighters who sought to free Kuwait from Iraq

Contents

Cover photo:
Kuwaiti men

CHAPTER

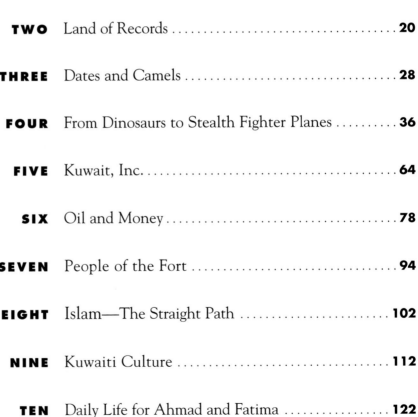

Fishing dhows in a
Kuwait harbor

A Kuwaiti camel

Kuwait at Risk

If you had been twelve-year-old Ahmad standing at the window of his Kuwait City home on August 2, 1990, you too might have been scared. Iraqi tanks were rumbling through the streets, and Iraqi helicopters were crisscrossing the sky above.

Ahmad was excited to see all the activity. He tried not to show any fear to his younger sister, Fatima, who was standing beside him. Her nursemaid, Rosa, who was from the Philippines, stood beside them trembling.

SOON HIS MOTHER ENTERED THE ROOM AND SHOOED THEM away from the window. Her tone of voice was edged with an unusual sharpness as she told them that their father had ordered them both to stay in their rooms, out of sight as much as possible. He was coming home with one of his American friends, whom they would try to hide.

Ahmad's father was in the oil industry. He had decided to remain in Kuwait in spite of the threats that Saddam Hussein, president of Iraq, was making against their country. His father said that he hoped that the Iraqis would have more respect for their Arab neighbors than to attack them. However, his father had no confidence in Saddam, whom he thought wanted to rule the whole Arab world and seize Kuwait and its oil.

Saddam Hussein

Ahmad's aunt and uncle, his cousins, and his older sister had left Kuwait for Egypt. If the news continued to be bad, they would go on to London to stay out of harm's way. They would look after the money the family had banked there.

When Ahmad's father returned home, his American friend, Jim, was already disguised in an Arab robe that

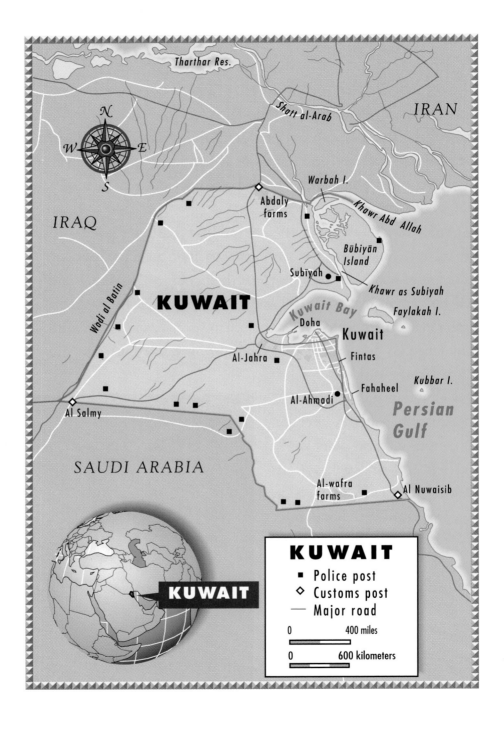

Geopolitical map of Kuwait

Tharthar Res.

Shatt al-Arab

IRAN

IRAQ

N
W E
S

Warbah I.

Abdaly
farms

Khawr Abd Allah

Būbiyān
Island

Subīyah

KUWAIT

Khawr as Subiyah

Kuwait Bay

Faylakah I.

Doha

Kuwait

Wadi al Batin

Al-Jahra

Fintas

Kubbar I.

Fahaheel

Al-Ahmadi

**Persian
Gulf**

Al Salmy

SAUDI ARABIA

Al-wafra
farms

Al Nuwaisib

KUWAIT

KUWAIT

■ Police post
◇ Customs post
— Major road

| 0 | 400 miles |

| 0 | 600 kilometers |

covered all of him except his face and shoes. Jim was given a bed in one of the servant's rooms. No one in the family was to discuss his presence. Ahmad's father announced that Jim would be moved soon to a safer location.

Then, Ahmad's father called the family together. He told them that Iraqi soldiers had forced him out of the car he was driving. He doubted that he would ever see it again. For now, it was important that the family not upset the Iraqi invaders in any way. Later, they would be able to help their country better if they were not suspected of giving trouble now.

That evening, the Iraqi soldiers came to Ahmad's home. His father offered them coffee and answered their questions. Thankfully, by then, Jim had been moved to another hiding place. The soldiers, however, took Rosa away for questioning.

When Rosa returned the next morning, she was crying. Her face was bruised. Ahmad's mother took her into her room to comfort her. Ahmad was glad that his older sister was with their aunt and uncle.

Ahmad's father sat down with him for a serious talk. He told Ahmad that he would have to be very careful about what he said and did. He gave Ahmad the names of three or four trusted relatives whom Ahmad could contact if anything happened to his father or mother. He told Ahmad that a number of people who had stayed in Kuwait intended to try to help their government. Their leaders had escaped to Saudi Arabia, a neighboring country to continue resisting the Iraqis with foreign help.

Ahmad had to be cautious in his contacts with friends in case one was a traitor. His father told him that he could help the resistance movement best of not angering the Iraqis. Then he would be freer to spy. Anyhow, with the large military presence, no one could challenge the soldiers directly. Those who tried were shot. Ahmad was to look after the family if his father had to be away from home or was taken by the Iraqis.

The next few days were difficult ones. His father went to his office where he was questioned. Ahmad, his sister, his mother, and Rosa stayed at home out of sight. A trusted servant went to the market to see about buying food. He reported that the market had

Vendors selling goods on the street

Kuwaitis lining up for food when supplies were short in March 1991

been bought out but that some of the merchants from whom they regularly purchased things had promised to save something for them tomorrow. He told them that people were frightened—but angry, too, at what the Iraqis were doing to them and their city. Ahmad's father warned the family to be careful not to use up their supplies quickly. If the crisis dragged on, they would need to use all their resources.

Ahmad stopped going to school and ran errands for his father. He kept his eyes open for anything that he thought would be useful to those who opposed the Iraqis. He started walking more—

A view of Kuwait City from the Persian Gulf

now that the family car had been taken. He picked up news in the markets. All this Ahmad reported back to his father, who passed it, along to his friends.

Saddam Hussein gave up trying to run the government through Kuwaiti puppets. He declared Kuwait a province of Iraq. As time passed, with the Iraqis still in control, Ahmad was trained to take a more active role in causing trouble for the soldiers. Once, he was assigned to slash the tires of an officer's car. Another time, he was told to create a disturbance in the market to distract the Iraqis. As Ahmad proved himself to be reliable and resourceful, he was given more difficult tasks. His father let him deliver some electronic equipment to a friend. Ahmad led a foreigner to a safer hiding place.

Ahmad heard the news of the buildup of Arab and Western forces in Saudi Arabia. Because Ahmad's father was a valuable person in the oil industry, the family was not hassled too much. Food and other things Ahmad had taken for granted, however, were no longer plentiful. His mother, along with other women, saw that medicine and food reached friends in need. Ahmad heard reports that the Iraqis had killed some animals in the zoo—one of his favorite places. Also, the soldiers were stripping equipment out of hospitals and shipping it to their country. Stories of what the Iraqis did to people who opposed them were played up on TV as a warning to others. Ahmad had seen with his own eyes some of the brutality. One of his best friends, Hassan, was tortured and killed by the soldiers.

Then on January 17, 1991, the news spread that the forces that had been building up in Saudi Arabia had bombed Baghdad, the capital of Iraq. The soldiers in Kuwait City seemed especially tense. Still, the Iraqis occupied the country.

Allied forces bombing Baghdad

Saddam spilled about 11 million barrels of oil into the Gulf waters bordering Kuwait City. The oil stuck on the rocks and sand of the shoreline, killed birds and fish, and created a stench in the air. After the war, Ahmad's father told him how some Kuwaitis had prevented an even greater flow by moving the controls from open to closed on some of the storage facilities and then changing the signs on the valves. That way the Iraqis were fooled into thinking that the tanks were draining.

Saddam was not finished, however. If he could not have the oil, no one would. He torched the Kuwaiti oil fields. Ahmad's father was furious. Here was Kuwait's wealth going up in smoke. It would be a tough fight to bring those fires under control.

Then on February 24, the U.S., Saudi, and Pan-Arab forces attacked through the Iraqi barrier system at the border of Kuwait. They encircled Kuwait City from the south and west and took the

Oil wells continued to burn even after the Iraqi troops left.

city and the airport. Ahmad was ordered to stay and protect his family.

What a relief it was when Kuwait was liberated on February 27, 1991! The Iraqis had tried to steal whatever was not tied down as they retreated. Ahmad saw dead Iraqi soldiers in the street, but he could not feel sorry for them. They had hurt his people and killed his friend, Hassan.

His father let him join in the celebration in the streets. As the allied forces that included American and Kuwaiti soldiers drove down the main street, there were shouts of joy. Kuwaiti citizens welcomed the liberating army by shooting off some of the hoarded ammunition. No longer were they forced to be Iraqis. They had their own country back.

Children returned to school as life got back to normal.

Soon, Ahmad's aunt, uncle, cousins, and older sister returned. Ahmad had many stories to tell them about what it was like to live through the Iraqi occupation. Funny, Ahmad thought. He seemed so much older than his cousin though they were the same age. He knew he would never forget the work he had done spying and taking care of his family. His father let him know how proud he was of the way Ahmad had acted.

Before long, Jim, the foreigner his father had rescued, returned to help with the cleanup in the oil fields. He expressed his gratitude to every member of Ahmad's family for saving his life. He brought presents for each of them.

Rosa, their nursemaid from the Philippines, was finally able to return to her family overseas. She wanted to leave before her contract to stay a year had ended. Ahmad's family understood her wish to return home. His father saw that she was well rewarded for the time she had spent with the family. He also told her that Iraq had to pay her compensation for her injuries and any losses. He cautioned, however, that Iraq might not be able to do so soon because of its financial problems.

Ahmad's life on the surface returned to what it was like before the Iraqi attack. He went back to school. He still thought much about what had happened in his life. Sometimes he woke out of a sound sleep frightened or angry because of memories of what he had seen. His little sister, Fatima, had lung problems, perhaps worsened by her breathing of the oil fumes.

Ahmad was proud of what his family had done to get rid of the Iraqis. He was much more serious than his cousin about what he wanted to do with his life. His father mentioned that it might be hard for the Kuwaitis who had suffered through the occupation to have the same trust in the Kuwaitis who had fled to safety in foreign countries. His uncle had served his family and his country well in London as part of the work of the Kuwaiti government-in-exile. His cousin had not taken any role in freeing Kuwait, however, and did not seem to appreciate how serious the danger was.

Now, years since the 1991 liberation, Ahmad still worries about Iraq's desire to take over his country. Saddam Hussein, Iraq's president, has several times since moved his troops toward Kuwait—only to be backed down again by the coalition forces including Kuwait, led by the United States. Ahmad wants Kuwait to be strong enough to fight off invasion attempts, but he knows his country would have difficulty doing that alone. Ahmad will do his service in the army and then continue his education as a petroleum engineer like his father. His sister plans to be a physician.

Cleanup began when the liberation was declared.

Land of Records

This small, rich desert country sits on a land that like a sponge is soaked with oil. The oil has been a blessing. Kuwait has used its wealth to achieve a high standard of living in a remarkably short period of time. The oil also has been a curse. It attracted the envy of Saddam Hussein, who invaded the country in 1990 and occupied it until armed forces of other nations, acting under the mandate of the United Nations, liberated Kuwait in 1991.

KUWAIT IS LOCATED ON THE NORTHWESTERN SHORE OF THE Arabian or Persian Gulf. Its eastern boundary is the Gulf. To the north and west is Iraq. On the southwest is Saudi Arabia. Across the Gulf is Iran. Kuwait owns several off-shore islands, the largest of which are Bubiyan, Faylakah, and Warbah. This roughly rectangular-shaped country contains approximately 6,880 square miles (17,818 sq km)—a little less than that of New Jersey or Wales.

Topographical map of Kuwait

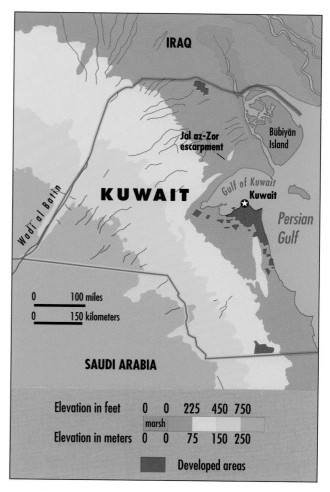

Desert on Oil

The land is generally flat or gently rolling with occasional low hills and shallow depressions. The elevation ranges from sea level on the east to almost 1,000 feet (305 m) in the southern part of the country.

Kuwaiti land can be roughly divided into four sections: (1) the dunes along the coast, (2) the salt marsh and salt depressions around Kuwait Bay, (3) a desert plateau in the west, and (4) the rest of the country that is desert with patches of coarse grasses.

Kuwait has rock outcrops, wadis (dry streambeds cut by water from the occasional rains), playas (desert basins that fill with water after the winter rains and provide

Geographical Features

Location: 28 degrees 32' to 30 degrees 6' N; 46 degrees 33' to 48 degrees 27' E

Area: Kuwait's undemarcated desert borders make its exact area uncertain, but the area is estimated at 6,880 square miles (17,818 sq km).

Highest point of elevation: A 900-foot (275-m) prominence in the southwest corner of the country and a 400-foot (120-m) ridge at Mina' al-Ahmadi provide the only breaks in Kuwait's stretches of desert and mud flats.

Lowest point of elevation: Sea level at the coastline

Temperatures: Summer temperatures range from 84°F (29°C) in the morning to 125°F (52°C) at midday and during the winter night temperatures occasionally reach the freezing point.

Annual average rainfall: 4 inches (10 cm)

Rivers: Kuwait has no major rivers or streams

Total boundary length: 598 miles (963 km)

Bordering countries and boundary lengths:

Saudi Arabia, 101 miles (163 km);
Iraq, 160 miles (257 km);
Persian Gulf shoreline, 132 miles (212 km)

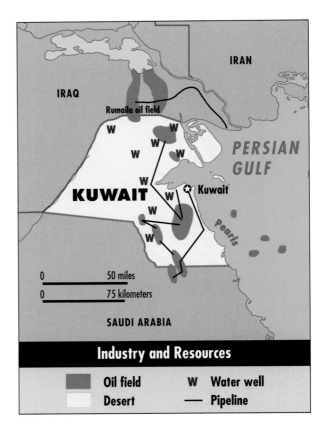

Industry and Resources

Oil field   W   Water well
Desert   —   Pipeline

An oil well in the Kuwaiti desert

Kuwaitis use the Gulf for many things, including fishing.

watering places for camel herds), and the Zor Hills (a slight elevation—a maximum of 425 feet, or 130 m—when the earth moved enough to break the plain and leave a scar).

At one time when the land masses were being formed, the whole Arabian peninsula is thought to have been joined to Africa. Indeed all the continents are supposed to have been jumbled together in patterns different from those we find on a map today. At some point, the continents broke apart and drifted away, sometimes knocking into each other. The Arabian peninsula is thought to have crashed up against Asia, tipping up the southwestern edge of Arabia and forming the Red Sea. As the land weathered, layers were sloughed off and washed down to the northeastern part of the peninsula, where Kuwait is located.

In addition to the great quantity of oil and natural gas beneath the land, there are small reservoirs of fresh water trapped between layers of rock. Most of the supply of drinking water, however, has to come from distilled sea water. In the past, water came by ship from the Shatt al-Arab waterway where the Tigris and Euphrates rivers discharge their supply of fresh water into the Gulf. No minerals have been found that could be exploited commercially. Even the sand is not marketable because it is very solid.

Kuwait's location on the Gulf is an asset. Historically, the Kuwaitis were a seafaring people who dove for pearls and had a thriving fishing industry. However, even before the 1991 war, overfishing and pollution threatened shrimp, the chief seafood export.

Saddam Hussein's Ecological Warfare

In just a few weeks, Saddam Hussein sent oil into the Gulf at an average rate of at least 150,000 barrels a day. The result was the biggest oil spill in history.

The oil did not immediately kill fish that live in the deep waters of the Gulf. The risk was that the chemicals from the oil might change the immune systems of the fish and lead to cancer. Then, if the smaller bait fish died off, the bigger fish would suffer.

The fish and birds along the shore of the Gulf were not so fortunate. The stickiness of the oil smothers things that it traps. Then the oil binds with the

sand and trapped animals sink. The Gulf has a wide shelf of shallow water along its coast. It has been very difficult to clean up this area.

The oil and soot from the Kuwait oil fires floated around the world. Scientists sampled air over Laramie, Wyoming, on March 25, 1991. Microscopic sulfuric acid droplets and carbon-rich soot particles were found to be ten times the normal amounts. Thunderstorms over India may have lofted the particles from Kuwait into the upper atmosphere. Then the jet stream could have sent them over Wyoming in just nine days.

A Climate That Sells Air Conditioners

The dry season between April and September finds the temperature usually up to 125°F (52°C) with an occasional record of 165°F (74°C). The winter months are better with temperatures that frequently are as high as 68°F (20°C). However, with a cold northwesterly wind in January the thermometer can drop to freezing at night with frost possible.

The annual rainfall averages from 1 to 7 inches (2.5 to 19 cm). The rain comes mostly between October and April when the desert may sprout a green grass cover that dies away in the hot, dry season. Cloudbursts can result in more than 2 inches (5.1 cm) of rain in a day.

Winds from the northwest are cool in winter and spring but hot in summer. Southeasterly winds that sometimes occur between July and October can be hot and damp. Hot and dry south winds are usual in spring and early summer. During winter, the tauz, a fierce dust storm sometimes lasting several days, can hit Kuwait.

Living in a Land of Records

Kuwait had shattered many records as an undeveloped country before the discovery of oil

Swimming is a good way to cool off on hot days in Kuwait.

Looking at Kuwaiti Cities

Al-Jahra is located 20 miles (32 km) west of Kuwait City and is a principal industrial and agricultural town. It is also the sight of the Red Fort, where the Kuwaitis suffered a siege by Islamic warriors from Saudi Arabia in 1920. The Red Fort is a celebrated national landmark.

Salimiyah is located to the east of Kuwait City, juts into the Arabian Gulf, and faces the island of Faylakah. It probably dates from around the same time as Kuwait City.

See chapter five for more information about Kuwait City.

A dust storm descending on Kuwait

led to its wealth today. The capital is one of the hottest, but also one of the most air-conditioned in the world. While blessed with a huge oil reserve, the country is short on water and had to build the world's biggest sea water distillation plant to get fresh water. During the Gulf War, the country suffered what has been called the greatest ecological disaster. Yet the fires that had been set in the oil fields during the Gulf War were extinguished sooner than anyone expected.

This solar energy plant was destroyed by the Iraqis.

A view of Kuwait's capital city

Dates and Camels

Considering the land and climate of Kuwait, it is surprising that the country has such a variety of plants and animals. Sometimes the variety has been achieved by importing foreign plants and animals and cultivating them.

Plants of the Desert

AS MANY AS 400 SPECIES OF FLORA HAVE BEEN COUNTED IN Kuwait. Kuwaitis have planted and watered European and to a lesser extent African plants in their yards.

The vegetation in the desert is mostly scrub and low bushes except during the short-lived grass of the spring season. Without sufficient water, seeds of plants may lie dormant for several seasons. When the plants do bloom, it is a time that Kuwaitis like to go out to the desert for picnics.

Camels, Horses, Falcons, and Other Animals

The Kuwaitis are proud of their desert heritage. They value camels, horses, and falcons both because of their past importance to people who needed to travel and hunt in this land and because of the sport they provide now.

Bedouin Caravan, by artist Richard Beavis

Camels were essential to the Bedouin, the people who traveled from place to place across the desert. Now more of the Bedouin have moved into the cities. The car and truck are more practical transportation in the desert in a country wealthy with oil. It is surprising then that ownership of camels has increased in spite of these trends. The people from town

Horse racing has been popular for Kuwaitis.

go out to visit their camels for a weekend holiday.

Arabian horses were proud possessions of the Bedouin. The upper classes in modern Kuwait breed and race horses as a hobby. Horses, however, were one of the casualties of the Iraqi invasion. Only seven of the thirty-two thoroughbreds at the ruler's stud farm remained alive in Kuwait. Some may have been taken away to Iraq. At the Equestrian Club in Kuwait City, forty-six of the one hundred twenty-two horses died of starvation. In the desert, some horses were found dead with their throats cut. Others were discovered barely alive and coated with the oily smoke of the wells set on fire by the Iraqis.

As many as three hundred species of birds have been counted

Date Palms—Traditional Source of Food for Desert Dwellers

Date palms grow to 60 feet (18 m) and have barbed leaves 9 feet (3 m) long. The female tree has branching spikes that can carry two hundred to a thousand dates each. The yield of a single tree can be 600 pounds (270 kg).

The trees bear fruit after eight years. They produce best between the 30th and 100th years. After that, they start to decline. The stalks and leaves can be woven, and the fiber can be used for rope.

Why Is the Camel So Good in the Desert?

The Kuwaiti camel, the one hump variety, is well designed for desert travel.

1. It can go great distances without water.
2. Its big feet do not sink into the sand.
3. It can provide milk and meat.
4. Its hair can be woven into cloth.
5. Its dung can be used for fuel.
6. It can bite off and eat thorny plants of the desert.
7. Its nostrils can close, and its eyelashes protect its eyes in sandstorms.
8. It can kneel down on the hot desert sand.
9. It can travel 100 miles (161 km) a day.
10. It can transport people and merchandise on its back.

in Kuwait. The birds stop off in Kuwait on a flight path between winter and summer homes. More than thirty types of birds of prey hunt the smaller birds and animals.

Falcons, one of these birds of prey, have been tamed by humans to be used for hunting. Falconry involves finding, training, and hunting these birds. At first, hunting was used to provide food for the members of the tribe. Falconry is also an exciting sport. Unfortunately, some modern hunters have not been sensitive to the need for conservation of the game.

Bird sanctuaries and the increasing supply of vegetation and water that existed before the Iraqi invasion helped to bring more birds into Kuwait. The oil spill, however, destroyed many shore feeding birds. It is estimated that at least 30,000 seabirds died as a direct result of the oil spill.

These Bedouin are selling a falcon.

Hunting accounts for the loss of the desert gazelle that used to roam wild but is now found only in zoos. With the use of modern guns and cars from which to shoot, hunters have extinguished some species from the wild. Desert foxes with their large ears, hedgehogs, jerboa, date bats, and occasionally wolves can be found in the desert. It is often difficult to study the desert animals that stay out of the hot sun and hunt at night.

The desert fox

Butterflies, moths, and dragonflies are attracted by the fresh water that can be found after their long flights over salt water and desert. Swarms of locusts used to be a danger to the limited vegetation available to the herds of sheep and goats. Efforts to wipe out these swarms seem to have this problem under control.

Spiders are common, including one that has the most powerful jaws of any animal for its size. Two types of scorpions that usually come out only at night can give painful bites. But they are not fatal, even to a child.

The desert is also home to poisonous snakes, such as the viper and the Arabian rear-fanged snake, and non-poisonous kinds, such as the sand boa. There are many kinds of lizards. The dhub, a spiny-tailed lizard, is considered good food. It changes color according to the season to attract or repel heat. It turns dark brown in winter and bright yellow in summer.

The sea was home to some kinds of poisonous sea snakes

This viper is one poisonous snake that lives in the desert.

Tragedy at the Zoo

Before the Gulf War, the Kuwait City Zoo (below) had about 442 animals. After liberation from the Iraqi occupation, only a few were found. Some were wandering in the oil fields, and others had been tortured or shot for food.

Two Kuwaiti brothers tried to help the animals during the period of occupation. Ali Mubarak al-Houti and his brother Suleiman had only occasionally visited the zoo before the war. However, they watched the Iraqis using the animals as targets. They tried to talk the soldiers out of shooting them by promising to bring them videos or cigarettes. Sometimes, the brothers talked the soldiers out of killing the animals. Other times, the brothers did not succeed.

The regular zoo employees fled in August 1990, when the Iraqis tried to force them to work for them. Before that time, Ali Mubarak had been a sanitary worker, and Suleiman, a security guard. Now they took over the work of the zookeepers. The two brought meat for the lions and tigers —the only animals that appeared healthy at liberation. Some of the animals—a giraffe, camel, Scottish Highland steer, monkeys, and baboons —roamed outside their cages.

After liberation, a representative of the World Society for the Protection of Animals reported that an elephant had a bullet wound in her shoulder. That organization bought 12,000 pounds (5,443 kg) of animal feed, and the St. Louis–based Purina Mills donated 8,000 pounds (2,629 kg) for the use of the zoo. The U.S. Army 100th Veterinary Medical Unit was on the scene trying to nurse the animals back to health (top right).

and to dolphin. Before the oil spill, some 300 species of fish were present in the area. The most popular fish used to be barracuda, king mackerel, subaitee, and harmour. These large fish feed on silversides, sardines, and anchovies. Ten species of shark used to swim in Gulf waters. Shrimp and mole lobster used to live at the bottom of the water. Four species of turtles that were considered endangered swam in these waters. It will take time for the Gulf to flush out the oil and rebuild animal life.

Even before the Gulf War, in 1978, the Kuwaitis hosted a conference to deal with the problems of pollution in Gulf waters in an attempt to get international action to head off the kind of damage that parts of Mediterranean Sea has suffered. Overfishing and pollution from new industrial activities were recognized as dangers then. Now with the massive oil spill, only time will tell how much the Gulf waters will recover.

A Saudi journalist holds two birds that were found dead on the oil-saturated shore.

From Dinosaurs to Stealth Fighter Planes

The history of Kuwait before 1700 reads like a good mystery story. The detective must deduce what happened from the clues discovered later. The oil underground, pottery pieces, a Greek-style temple, written documents from other parts of the world—these are the clues that the historian uses to tell the early story of Kuwait.

THE GREAT OIL RESERVE WAS LAID DOWN DURING THE Mesozoic Era (70 to 225 million years ago). During a 60-million-year period in the last stages of that era, the earth had abundant vegetation and animal life, such as the dinosaurs. The sea level must have fluctuated with the climate changes of the ice ages. Areas now underwater are thought to have been once dry land. About 15,000 B.C., the Arabian Gulf may have been a dry basin down to the Strait of Hormuz.

Early Human Records

The first clues about humans are found in flints, tools, and weapons fashioned by people from easily worked stone. This evidence may date from about 6,000 B.C. Pottery begins in the eastern Arabian Peninsula about 5,000 B.C.

Ruins on Faylakah Island

The great Sumerian civilization along the Tigris and Euphrates rivers was located to the north of Kuwait. On the Kuwaiti island of Faylakah, archaeologists (scientists who explore early history) found seals, pottery, burials, and buildings associated with a civilization dating from 2200 B.C.

Was Dilmun in Kuwait?

Dilmun might have been just a mythical place. It was mentioned in early writings as a place from which there was trade in copper, lumber, incense, and precious stones such as lapis lazuli and carnelian. It was noted in one of the world's earliest surviving stories, *The Epic of Gilgamesh*. But did Dilmun exist?

Danish scientists were called in to explore the island of Faylakah in 1957. They found pottery that indicated settlements during the Dilmun and ancient Greek Hellenistic periods. The town plans, the name of a god discovered on a bowl, and the pottery made the archaeologists think that they had found a link to the ancient civilizations to the north such as the Babylonians. However, the weights and measures of this trading nation were those of the Indus civilization to the east and not the northern Babylonians. What had they found?

Geoffrey Bibby, the English field director for the expedition by the Danish Prehistoric Museum of Aarhus, tells in his book *Looking for Dilmun* what it was like to work in Bahrain, Kuwait and other places on the Arabian Peninsula.

The archaeologists came up with a Greek inscription on stone: "Stoles, the Athenian, and the soldiers . . . to Zeus, the Savior, to Poseidon, and to Artemis, the Savioress." What was a Greek from far away Athens doing on the island of Faylakah?

Alexander the Great (356–323 B.C.) marched with his Greek soldiers to build an empire that extended from Egypt and into Persia and India. The conqueror had intended to make Babylon one of the capitals of his new empire. Instead, he died there of a fever when he was only thirty-three years old. His empire was divided up among his generals, and the territory that is now Kuwait came under Greek control from the fourth to first centuries B.C.

Alexander the Great

About A.D. 170, a Roman historian, Arrian, wrote an account of Alexander's conquests. According to this source, a Greek admiral named Nearchos sailed up the Indus River and explored the Arabian coastline on his return journey. Nearchos described in a report an island that may well have been Faylakah.

With the defeat of the Greeks by the Romans, Kuwait sank back into mystery. Some ancient writers and some coins indicate that there may have been a small state at the head of the Arabian Gulf, but the exact location is unknown. By the third century, Christianity arrived in this part of the world. A monastery and church have been found on nearby Kharg Island, now owned by Iran.

Muhammad and Islam

Around A.D. 570, in the city of Mecca on the Arabian Peninsula to the southwest of Kuwait, Muhammad was born. He was to become the prophet of Islam, the religion followed by Kuwaitis today.

After Muhammad's death in 632, the new religion spread rapidly among the Arabian tribes to challenge the Ottoman and Persian empires. A battle between the early Islamic troops and the Persians was fought at a place near the head of the Gulf. Some historians believe the battle may have been at Kadhima on the north shore of Kuwait Bay.

The Persian commander thought that he would have an easy victory and brought with him chains to bind the Arab prisoners. Instead, he was defeated, and the Arabs acquired a great quantity of goods. The fight came to be called the "Battle of the Chains."

The Arab forces were led by the great Khalid, known as "the sword of Allah."

Power in the Islamic Empire shifted from Mecca and Medina, in what is now Saudi Arabia, to Damascus, in what is now Syria, and then to Baghdad, in what is now Iraq. Power in the Empire splintered among various local family rulers. The Mongols from the east held power from 1258 to 1546 after which the Ottoman Turks took control from 1546 to 1918. These empires did not exert much direct power over the area around Kuwait.

From 1507 to 1650, the Portuguese occupied and dominated the Arabian Gulf. Portugal was a great seafaring nation that had sent Vasco da Gama around the Cape of Good Hope in Africa. The Portuguese fought the Ottomans, built fortresses, and noted Kuwaiti place names on their maps. The British took over an interest in the territory after the Portuguese power waned.

The Sabah Family and the Sheikdom

Early in the eighteenth century, Bedouin from central Arabia were perhaps driven by a drought to find water and pasture for their animals elsewhere. They found fresh water on the southern shore of Kuwait Bay. These people were known as the Bani Utub, meaning "the people who moved, or trekked." Among them were the forebears of the Sabah family, who were to rule Kuwait; the Kalifah family, who were to rule Bahrain; and the Ghanim, Shemlan, and Saleh families, who were to become important merchants.

Because the site had a source of drinking water, some fishing families must have been living there already. The territory was supposedly under the control of the Bani Khalid, a powerful tribe of northeast Arabia. On Western maps the area would have been shown as part of the Ottoman Empire, but the Ottomans exercised little control of the area.

The name Kuwait means "fort" or, perhaps in a fuller translation of the Arabic word, "little fortress on a hill near the water." The newcomers needed to be able to protect themselves. They also used diplomatic channels. According to one tradition, about the middle of the eighteenth century, the Kuwaitis sent a delegation to the Ottomans at Basra (now in Iraq) to explain that they desired to live in peace. The head of that mission was Sabah I, who was acknowledged as the sheik, or the leader of the tribe. Ever since then the sheik has been chosen from a member of the Sabah family. The office does not necessarily pass from father to son but may go to a brother or another relative who is considered by the family to be the best leader. The Sabah tribe made peace with the stronger Bani Khalid tribe by marrying their daughters.

The earliest record of the new settlement

A Bedouin messenger

A caravan of Arabian merchants

The Al-Sabah Dynasty of Kuwait

(From 1899–1961 Kuwait was under British administration)

1756–1764 Sabah I, the first ruler of Kuwait, initiates the al-Sabah dynasty, which still rules Kuwait today

1764–1815 Abdullah I

1815–1859 Jaber I

1859–1866 Sabah II

1866–1892 Abdullah II

1892–1896 Muhammad

1896–1915 Mubarak "the Great"

1915–1917 Jaber II

1917–1921 Salim

1921–1950 Ahmad

1950–1965 Abdullah III

1965–1977 Sabah III

1977–   Jaber III

comes from a Danish traveler, Carsten Neibuhr, who visited Kuwait in 1765. He reported that the inhabitants lived by fishing and pearl diving with more than eight hundred boats. In the season for good sailing winds, the town was almost deserted, with everyone out on fishing or trading trips.

Kuwait became an important trade center. The British East India Company began to use Kuwait for its system of communications. Fast mail could be carried across the desert to Aleppo on the Mediterranean by camel riders in fourteen to twenty days. Camel caravans transporting goods took about eighty days. These caravans often consisted of some five thousand camels and one thousand men.

In Arabia, a fighting force of Bedouin had formed who were dedicated to the purification and reform of Islam. They believed that their religion had been contaminated by outside practices. These people followed a religious leader called Mohammed bin Abdul Wahhab. These Wahhabis came from central Arabia and attacked Kuwait with raids and threats. The rulers of

The original arms of the East India Company

Kuwait called on the help of the British-backed East India Company. The Company brought cannons and men to counter five hundred of the Wahhabis. The Wahhabis retaliated by intercepting the Company's mail carriers, forcing the abandonment of Kuwait as a mail route.

The early part of the nineteenth century was also a time of pirate attacks by sea. One of the most famous of the pirates was a Kuwaiti, Rahma ibn Jabir, who, with a fleet of five or six ships, was able to harass Gulf shipping for more than twenty years. The prosperity of Kuwait declined during this period of uncertainty until the British Navy brought peace to the Gulf by 1860.

The Sabah rulers had the difficult task of governing two groups with quite different interests: the merchants of the town and the Bedouin of the desert. The population of the town was more numerous and provided the wealth of the royal family. Peace was important to the prosperity of the merchants. Bedouin attacks could hurt business.

Although less numerous and poorer, the Bedouin had great prestige as the embodiment of the desert traditions of honor, courage, and hospitality. The Sabah family maintained close ties with these desert fighters. The Sabah followed the custom of desert sheiks holding sessions during which even the humblest of the people could approach them with their problems. They took wives from among the women of the noble tribes and sent their sons to live among the Bedouin and learn desert ways.

Camels were used for transporting goods.

Rahma ibn Jabir

This is modern-day Kuwait City. This city became a summer resort at the turn of the century.

The Sabah family was also sensitive to foreign power. They maintained good relations with the Ottoman Turks, but also cultivated the British when they thought the Turks were threatening to occupy Kuwait. The British were glad to oblige with protection in order to keep the Germans from claiming influence in the territory. Kuwaiti frontiers were drawn in a treaty between Turkey and Great Britain in 1913 that was not ratified because of the start of World War I in 1914.

During the reign of Sheik Mubarak the Great from 1896 to 1915, Kuwait changed from being a sheikdom without a defined status to becoming an autonomous state backed by the British. Kuwait prospered under Mubarak. Kuwait City became a kind of summer resort for people of the area. Although the climate was hot, it was dry and healthy in contrast to the damp air around Basra, Iraq, where the danger of malaria was great. Mubarak invited U.S. missionaries to open a medical station in Kuwait. The Arabian mission of the Dutch Reformed Church in America provided medical service in Kuwait from 1911 until the oil wealth permitted Kuwait to build its own hospitals.

Mubarak the Great

Mubarak came to power in a palace coup. His half-brother, who was the ruler, was weak and under the influence of a pro-Turkish adviser. Mubarak was sent out to subdue the Bedouin tribes that had a "protection racket"—"take our protection or else risk what we will do to you"—for anyone traveling to or from Kuwait City. He may have been aware that he was being sent away to be killed because his half-brother gave him no funds for this task.

Mubarak, a forceful personality and knowledgeable about desert ways, won the backing of several of the strong tribal leaders. When no funds were given him, Mubarak decided that the only way to do what was needed was for him to kill his brother and seize power.

With a handful of followers that

included his two young sons, he rode with the others on the swiftest camels to the palace. Just before midnight of May 17, 1896, Mubarak climbed up on the roof of the palace where he knew his brother would be sleeping and killed him.

The servants were not allowed to leave the palace to give any warning. The next morning, when it was the custom for the ruler to be available to anyone who wanted to see him, Mubarak was seated in his brother's seat. When the room was full, Mubarak drew his sword and laid it across his knee. He announced the death of his brother and his rule and he then invited any comments. Of course, there were none. When the news was carried to the streets, crowds came to acclaim Mubarak as the ruler.

Mubarak sided with Britain and the Allies in World War I, and, in return, the British promised that Mubarak's five date gardens in Iraq would be free of all taxes, that his title to the gardens would be upheld, and that his family would be maintained as sheiks of Kuwait forever by the British government. After the British government in Iraq ended in 1961, the Iraqis did not consider themselves bound by the British promises.

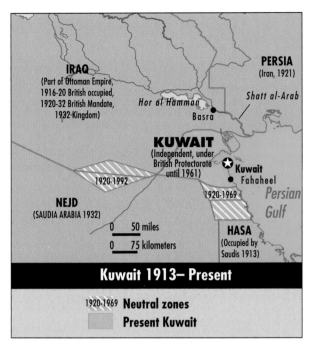

IRAQ
(Part of Ottoman Empire,
1916-20 British occupied,
1920-32 British Mandate,
1932 Kingdom)

Hor al Hamman

Basra

PERSIA
(Iran, 1921)

Shatt al-Arab

KUWAIT
(Independent, under
British Protectorate
until 1961)

Kuwait
Fahaheel

1920-1992

1920-1969

Persian
Gulf

NEJD
(SAUDIA ARABIA 1932)

0   50 miles

0   75 kilometers

HASA
(Occupied by
Saudis 1913)

Kuwait 1913– Present

1920-1969 **Neutral zones**

Present Kuwait

Mubarak had protected the Saud family that came from central Arabia when it had been ousted by its enemies. When that tribe returned and ruled what is now Saudi Arabia, relations with the Saudis were good. Mubarak's son, Sheik Salim, however, created tension with the Saudis by giving shelter to an enemy tribe. It was at this point that Mubarak died, and Kuwait lost his close relationship to the Saudis. Salim later became ruler and was attacked by Saudi forces. The British let it be known that an attack on Kuwait would be an attack on Britain.

The death of Sheik Salim helped to ease tensions, but it was clear that some decision about boundary disputes would have to be taken. The British presided at the Conference of Uqair in 1922, which set some dividing lines among the parties. The Saudis and Iraq claimed much of the same land. The Saudis claimed all of Kuwait. The new borders gave a large territory claimed by the Saudis to Iraq and then gave nearly two-thirds of Kuwaiti territory to the Saudis. Neutral zones where it was thought that oil might be discovered were established to which the two countries had an equal claim. (These zones existed until the boundary settlement approved by the United Nations in 1992.) The Kuwaitis were not happy, but they were helpless to counter the British action.

Sheik Ahmad and Oil Development

Sheik Ahmad became the new ruler of Kuwait upon Salim's death. A Saudi blockade of trade and the world depression in the years after 1929 caused financial problems in Kuwait. Raids into Kuwait by tribesmen did not always have the Saudi leader's backing. When such an attack was made in 1928, Sheik Ahmad commandeered all available cars in Kuwait. Fifteen cars were able to intercept and attack the raiders in what was the first desert battle in which motor vehicles were used. Thanks to this innovation, the Kuwaitis defeated the raiders and took their loot.

It was under Sheik Ahmad that the basis of the oil industry was established. After prospecting revealed the potential of this resource, the sheik granted a joint concession in 1934 to Gulf Oil of the United States and Anglo Persian Oil of Great Britain. They formed the Kuwait Oil Company, Ltd., and started deep drilling in 1936. This work was just beginning to be productive when World War II began in 1939. The oil wells were plugged in 1942, and drilling was stopped until after the war.

The Kuwait Oil Company was owned by British and U.S. companies.

When the petroleum industry boomed after the war, Kuwait City changed from being a small Gulf port to becoming a growing modern city. Before the concession agreement was signed, the British Political Officer Lt. Col. H. R. P. Dickson warned the sheik

A Kuwaiti crowd in Kuwait City demonstrating their support of the Iraqi regime in 1962

Kuwait became a member of the United Nations in 1963.

of the great changes that would come to his country with wealth. Sheik Ahmad replied: "I must do this for my people, even if it will bring undesirable things to my country. We are poor, pearling is not what it used to be, so I must sign."

Modern Times

Sheik Ahmad was the last of the traditional rulers. Sheik Abdullah, who succeeded him, was to bring changes to Kuwait in both the political and economic spheres. The treaty of 1961 with Great Britain ended the protectorate and established Kuwaiti independence.

Six days after the treaty with Great Britain was signed, the Iraqis declared that Kuwait was Iraqi territory and that the ruler, now called the emir, should not obstruct the Iraqis. The emir asked the British for support, and they sent in troops. The Arab League (an organization of Arab countries) met and agreed to send in Arab armed forces to replace the British troops. Saudi Arabia, Jordan, the United Arab Republic (at that time a union between Egypt and Syria), and the Sudan supplied armed forces.

Kuwait became a member of the United

Kuwait's Pearl

Before oil was the basis of Kuwait's wealth, pearls had been the great prize. When Sheik Ahmad visited London, he took with him the largest pearl ever found in Kuwait as a gift to Queen Mary of the United Kingdom. It was perfectly round and flawless, the size of a marble. For security, the sheik's personal bodyguard, a man named Mirjan, carried the pearl in his mouth. Mirjan had to eat breakfast, however, so he took the pearl out and put it on a dressing table in his hotel room. When he finished eating, he went to replace the pearl in his mouth, but the gift was missing. When the Kuwaitis reported their loss, a chambermaid who had found it under the bed returned the pearl, saying that she thought it was a bead of no value.

Sheik Sabah

Sheik Jaber

Nations on May 14, 1963. By October of that year, with a change in government in Iraq, Iraq announced a decision to recognize Kuwait's complete independence. In return, it is thought that Kuwait made a substantial financial grant to Iraq.

Sheik Abdullah died on November 14, 1965, having ruled during the time that Kuwait was recognized as a fully functioning nation. His rule was taken over by Sheik Sabah, with Sheik Jaber being named the heir apparent, or crown prince, in May 1966.

Sheik Sabah continued to be neutral for the most part in disputes among Arab nations. In the 1967 Arab war with Israel, Kuwait joined in the oil embargo on the United States and the United Kingdom, nations who were supporting Israel. Kuwait gave financial assistance to the United Arab Republic (now Egypt) and Jordan as well as the Palestine guerrilla fighters. This support helped to blunt the criticism of radical Arabs against

Kuwait as a rich, privileged nation. The large Palestinian population in Kuwait—about 350,000 of some of the most able and best-educated Palestinians—was one of the reasons for the strong Kuwaiti backing of Palestinian organizations.

Meanwhile, on the domestic front, the people appreciated the public programs and land compensation projects that had been financed through money from the oil industry. These policies resulted in a distribution of income to a wider circle of Kuwaitis. However, people criticized the corruption and inefficiency of the public officials. Also, they complained about government manipulation of the public press and the legislature. To counter this discontent, the Sabah family permitted an election of the legislature, and a committee was formed to review the constitution.

On the international front in 1973, Iraq again threatened with troops occupying the Kuwaiti outpost at Samtah. The troops withdrew, but Iraq claimed the Kuwaiti Bubiyan Island. As a result of this crisis, Kuwait expanded its armed forces, established a navy, and approved legislation for compulsory service in the armed forces.

In the Arab–Israeli war of October 1973, Kuwait sent troops and gave financial aid to other Arab states. It tried to pressure Western countries to force an Israeli withdrawal from occupied Arab territory by limiting oil exports. In 1975, Kuwait almost completely nationalized the oil industry.

Sheik Sabah died on December 31, 1977, and was succeeded by his cousin, Sheik Jaber, with the new crown prince, Sheik Saad. In the war between Iraq and Iran that began in 1980, Kuwait supported Iraq with money and access to ports. Iran, with its radical leadership of Shiite Muslims (the second largest branch of Islam), posed a threat to the Sabah family of Sunni Muslims (the largest branch of Islam). In 1981, Kuwait joined with Saudi Arabia, the United Arab Emirates, Qatar, Oman, and Bahrain as a founding member of the Gulf Cooperation Council (GCC) with the hope of increasing the cooperation and security of the small oil-producing countries along the Gulf.

Iran did not like Kuwait's support of Iraq in the Iran–Iraq war (1980–1988). Bombing of oil installations, Kuwait City, and Kuwaiti oil tankers, and a hijacking of a Kuwaiti plane were thought to be the work of Shiite Muslims inspired by Iran. An attempt to assassinate the emir by driving a car bomb into a procession of cars resulted in a crackdown on those who were thought to be behind the attacks. In 1985 and 1986, almost 27,000 people, many Iranian, were deported.

In 1986 and 1987, Iran seized merchant ships sailing to and from Kuwait and took their cargoes. Kuwait countered by registering most of its oil fleet as American, Liberian, British, or Russian. It received help with mine sweeping operations from the United States, Saudi Arabia, France, Britain, the Netherlands, Belgium, and Italy. Iran continued its attacks on Kuwaiti territory.

Many foreign citizens lived in Kuwait. The country adopted a program of "Kuwaitization" designed to achieve a majority of Kuwaitis in the population by 2000. This policy would not be easy to put into effect because the majority of the people in industry were foreigners.

By July 1990, Saddam Hussein was criticizing countries for exceeding their oil production quotas approved by the

A Kuwaiti looks at the palace after it was damaged by the Iraqis.

Organization of Petroleum Exploring Countries (OPEC) and accusing Kuwait of stealing $2.4 billion of Iraqi oil reserves. Iraq then announced that Kuwait should cancel Iraq's war debt and compensate Iraq for losses sustained during that country's eight year war with Iran. Arab leaders were alarmed by the charges, including the demand for territory, that Iraq was pressing on Kuwait. They tried to mediate a resolution without success.

Iraq invaded Kuwait on August 2, 1990. The emir and crown prince escaped to set up a government in exile in Saudi Arabia. Their brother tried to defend the palace with troops but was killed.

His soldiers were slaughtered after a surrender. Iraq invaded with 100,000 troops; Kuwait's total military strength was only 20,000. Iraq had the largest armed force in the region and was twenty-seven times the size and nine times the population of Kuwait.

Kuwaiti citizens were killed, raped, and tortured. Sometimes they were brought to be killed in front of the homes of their family. Stores were looted. Homes and private bank accounts were taken. No one was safe—not the Kuwaitis, not the foreign workers, and certainly not the members of the Sabah family whom Saddam Hussein had targeted.

Inside Kuwait, citizens organized resistance. When women and children marched in protest of the invasion, they were shot. Graffiti appeared on the wall of the palace: "We are all Jaber and Saad" (referring to the emir and crown prince). "We are all for Kuwait, and we want no one except them."

Meanwhile the international community took action. On August 3, the day after the invasion, the United Nations and the Arab League condemned the Iraqi aggression. Iraq responded by setting up a provisional nine-member government for Kuwait claiming that it was simply responding to the call for help from Kuwaiti citizens. On August 6, the United Nations instituted economic sanctions. The next day Saudi Arabia

These Syrian troops joined the forces in Saudi Arabia to fight the Iraqi forces.

invited troops from other nations to help defend that country. Iraq countered with disbanding the provisional Kuwaiti government, announcing the takeover of Kuwait, and ordering foreign embassies there to close. The United Nations adopted a resolution declaring Iraq's annexation void.

Why had Saddam Hussein risked the attack on Kuwait? Kuwait had three things that he wanted: oil, wealth, and Gulf ports. If he had succeeded, he would have controlled 20 percent of the world's oil supply. Industrial nations would have had to give in to his demands. He would have secured the substantial wealth of Kuwaiti reserve funds. He would have gained valuable Gulf ports, particularly important because Iraqi ports had been damaged by Iran during the previous war.

And Saddam Hussein would have been seen as the great leader of the Arabs.

Because the United States and the Soviet Union were cooperating, the United Nations was able to try to keep the peace without the interference that had been present during the era of conflict between these two nations. A coalition of twenty-eight nations, including a number of Arab countries, worked together to set up a defensive Desert Shield to prevent Iraq from pushing into other Gulf states. Kuwaiti soldiers and pilots fought with the coalition.

Saddam Hussein did not respond to diplomatic efforts to get him to withdraw. The night of January 16, 1991, was clear and

Opposite: **A soldier surveying the zone between Kuwait and Iraq**

An aerial view of the U.N. headquarters at the Kuwait-Iraq border at the end of the war

dark—perfect for the air war. The military operation known as Desert Shield turned into Desert Storm, as United States General Norman Schwarzkopf told the coalition forces that they would be the thunder and lightning of the war to get Saddam Hussein out of Kuwait. The airfields shook with the noise and vibrations of planes taking off on their bombing raids on Baghdad, the capital of Iraq.

The ground war was not to begin until late February. Then Kuwaiti soldiers fought alongside the Egyptians and other Arabs on the border between Kuwait and Saudi Arabia. As the armed

Surrendering Iraqi soldiers

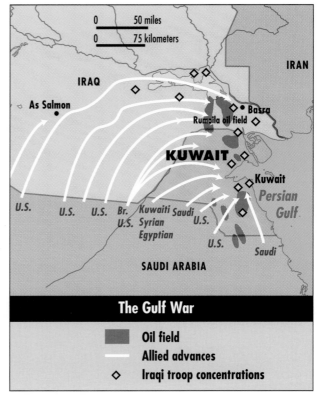

The Gulf War

- Oil field
- Allied advances
- ◇ Iraqi troop concentrations

General Schwarzkopf's Farewell Speech to Some U.S. Troops

The general (seated at left) cautioned his soldiers about telling war stories: "Don't ever forget to say in your story there were Kuwaitis, Omanis, French Foreign Legion protecting our right flank, with Egyptian forces involved, because you were part of the great coalition—the great coalition of forces determined not to let a petty dictator, no matter what size his army, no matter how many tanks he had, no matter how many men he had armed— despite the fact you were badly outnumbered, you were determined to show a petty dictator that they just can't get away with bullying neighbors and taking what they want because they think they are so tough."

forces cleared paths through the minefields and defensive barriers into Kuwait, many Iraqi soldiers surrendered. Intense fighting was centered at the Kuwait Air Field. Coalition forces, however, surprised the Iraqis by moving troops far to the west in the desert, only 150 miles (240 km) from Baghdad, to encircle their army.

Iraqis fled Kuwait City in 1991, causing a huge traffic jam. These burned-out vehicles littering the road are the aftermath of U.S. bombing.

The rout of Iraqi troops involved another round of looting and taking hostages by the retreating soldiers. Iraqis killed people senselessly. Some Kuwaitis who had been tortured before were killed to prevent their giving evidence. Buildings and facilities were destroyed. A huge traffic jam on the road leading out of Kuwait developed as Iraqis and their collaborators commandeered cars, piled them high with looted TVs and other goods and took hostages with them. These Iraqis were exposed to the final bombing and strafing raids.

On February 27, 1991, U.S. president George Bush announced that Kuwait had been liberated, the Iraqi army had been defeated, and coalition forces were suspending offensive combat operations

100 hours after the beginning of ground operations and six weeks since the start of Desert Storm. With liberation after seven months of occupation, the people of Kuwait celebrated, dancing in the streets, firing off their guns, and welcoming the coalition forces. They also took out some of their anger on persons who had collaborated with the Iraqis and had harmed their families. Desert Storm was over, but the Kuwaitis faced a tremendous task in rebuilding their country.

Crowds of Kuwaitis gathered in the streets to welcome liberation.

Troops from many countries celebrated the victory.

With the chaotic state in which the nation was left, martial law was declared. Weapons of all kinds were readily available. Basic services such as electricity and desalinated water had been disrupted. Money had to be checked carefully for serial numbers since Kuwaiti bills looted by the Iraqis had been declared invalid. The air was darkened by the smoke and ash of the oil well fires.

The government needed skilled people and encouraged more Kuwaitis to work. They did not want widespread return of foreign technicians or unskilled labor. The government aimed for a population of 1.2 million people, two-thirds of whom would be Kuwaiti. This goal represented a continuation of the Kuwaitization prewar policy.

The Iraqis stole $20 billion in gold,

foreign currency, jewelry, cars, trucks, computers, household items, and medical equipment. The Kuwaitis hired experts to try to trace some of these losses. In addition, the Iraqis did at least $25 billion in damages to buildings, roads, desalination plants, oil wells, refineries, and pipelines. The United Nations decided that Iraq would be expected to pay a percent of its future oil revenues into a compensation fund for victims of its invasion including environmental damage, loss of Kuwaiti revenue from the oil wells, loss of wages to foreigners who fled, and other property damage. The first payout from this fund was not until 1994, however.

The physical rebuilding of Kuwait has been amazingly quick. Yet the country has been deeply affected by the occupation and by the continuing threats of Saddam Hussein. In August 1992, he again claimed that Kuwait was an Iraqi province. The United Nations Security Council, however, accepted the borderlines its commission had drawn.

In 1993, Iraq sent workers into the demilitarized zone to retrieve Silkworm antiship missiles left in the area granted to Kuwait. The United States and the United Nations responded by sending in more security forces. Iraqi protesters threatened

Iraqis looted stores and businesses during their invasion.

Opposite: **The air remained dark due to smoke and ash.**

Two U.S. citizens speaking with an Arab about rebuilding war-torn Kuwait

Madeleine Albright, U.S. ambassador to the U.N., giving a speech in 1994 as Iraqi troops move to the Kuwaiti border

UNITED STATES

Kuwaiti workers digging a long security trench along the border. Also, in that year, there was an assassination plot attributed to Iraq against U.S. President George Bush, who was visiting Kuwait.

In 1994, Iraq moved 20,000 of its crack troops to within 20 miles (30 km) of the border to join 50,000 of the regular troops there. The United States sent troops to Kuwait, and the United Nations condemned the Iraqi action. In response, Iraq said it recognized Kuwait as a nation and respected its borders.

In 1995, U.S. ambassador to the United Nations Madeleine Albright displayed satellite photos showing some 9,000 items of military hardware that the Iraqis had seized during the 1990 occupation and were using against orders of the United Nations. Two of Saddam Hussein's family who had escaped to Jordan reported that Iraq had planned an attack on Kuwait in August. Iraq replied that the reports were "merely a frog's croaking."

In 1996, the Iraqis fired missiles at two U.S. jets policing the no-fly zone. U.S. President Bill Clinton responded by sending F-117 stealth fighters to Kuwait. Iraq called the Kuwaiti action of basing the fighters on their territory an act of aggression. The U.S. State Department spokesperson stated that the core of U.S. strategic interests involves the protection of Saudi Arabia and Kuwait.

Meanwhile on the domestic front, Kuwaiti rulers were permitting some reforms of democratic process for its citizens. Although there was protest that the government was not moving fast enough, there was also a conservative Islamic faction that did not want to see the adoption of some Western ideas and practices. Nevertheless, the elections and the accountability of the government to its citizens put Kuwait ahead of other Gulf countries in achieving the reform goals in some measure.

New construction in the days after liberation

Kuwait, Inc.

In the West, the nickname of Kuwait, Incorporated, was tagged to the country because before the war Kuwait had an estimated $100 billion in foreign investments. The country seemed to be run like a family business for the profit of the Sabah family—a family of more than 1200 members.

To the Bedouin mind, the emir was acting just like the sheik of a large tribe who has responsibility for his family's welfare and for seeing that his tribe prospered. The tribe is not run democratically, with everyone having an equal vote. On the other hand, the sheik does not have unlimited power and is expected to consult the elders of the family about important matters.

When the oil wealth started rolling in, the emir had to deal with his family responsibilities and traditional ways, but he also had to contend with the Western ideas that business leaders and his young people were bringing into Kuwait. It is not surprising that the changes from a poor to a rich nation should cause problems in the culture. Even so, Kuwait is a leader among the Gulf nations in establishing democratic structures.

Government

Kuwait is a constitutional monarchy. The constitution was adopted on November 16, 1962. In 1976, the emir (the monarch) suspended certain articles dealing with the National Assembly (called the Majlis al-Umma). Then in 1980, the emir issued a decree calling for an elected National Assembly. In 1986 after a number of terrorist acts, the emir did away with requirements that new elections for the Assembly be held within two months of his dismissing the legislature. There have been new elections in

The National Assembly building in Kuwait City

A crowd celebrating after the 1992 election

1992, however, and again in 1996. The constitution provides that the sovereignty of Kuwait may not be surrendered. Its territory may not be given away. Offensive war is prohibited.

The emir must be an heir of the famed Mubarak. He is chosen by the members of the ruling family. He must appoint a crown prince, or heir apparent, within one year of taking office. Also, he appoints the prime minister "after the traditional consultations." To date, the crown prince and the prime minister have been the same person although some reformers hoped the two offices would be separated.

Flag and Emblem

After Kuwait became a recognized nation in 1961, it adopted a flag (right) and emblem. The flag has green, white, and red stripes with a black trapezoid at the edge on the staff. The green is the color of paradise, special for Islam. The white is for the achievements of the nation. Red symbolizes the future; and the black is for the battlefields. The emblem shows a dhow (boat) in full sail encircled by a falcon with the words Dowlat al Kuwait, which means "Kuwait independent."

The emir appoints and dismisses members of the Council of Ministers (cabinet) on the recommendation of the prime minister. These persons need not be members of the Assembly although they become members automatically for as long as they serve on the Council. Ministers may not sell property to the government. To hold a government job, a person must be a Kuwaiti citizen.

The emir also can formulate laws and establish public institutions. The laws must be published in the *Official Gazette*. All decrees must be sent to the Assembly. No law is issued unless approved by the Assembly.

The Assembly has fifty members elected for a four-year term subject to the possibility of the emir dismissing the legislature before then. Only Kuwaiti males over the age of twenty-one years may vote. Women, servicemen, and police do not have voting rights. In 1994, the Assembly decided to allow sons of naturalized Kuwaitis to vote. In 1995, the Assembly dropped the period in which naturalized Kuwaitis had to wait to become eli-

Sheik Jaber, Emir of Kuwait

Because Arabic names list the parentage of the person, the sheik's name is Jaber al-Ahmad al-Jaber al-Sabah. He was born in 1928 and was educated in Kuwaiti schools and with private tutors. As permitted under Islamic law, he has four wives. He has some forty children. His hobby is growing roses.

Sheik Jaber became emir in 1977 when Sheik Sabah died of a heart attack. Jaber had been serving as crown prince and prime minister. In the 1950s, the British had picked him out as a likely ruler. He was an active prime minister and had taken on many tasks because the emir's ill health had forced him to turn over almost all except the ceremonial role. Therefore, it was easy for Jaber to become the head of state.

Jaber was well liked. He was a hard worker. Unlike many Kuwaitis who escape to cooler climates during the summer heat, Jaber remained in Kuwait during the summer months.

The big question was whom he would choose to be crown prince and prime minister. There are two main branches of the Sabah family that have produced the rulers: the Jaber and the Salim. Often the post was alternated between the two although Jaber, himself, had been passed over when a Salim emir followed a Salim.

Saad, on the Salim side, had studied police work in England. He had served as a deputy police chief, minister of the interior, and minister of defense. Another Salim was Jaber Ali, who had been an acting prime minister and an information minister. He had powerful support from the Bedouin through his mother's tribe. Both men were older than the emir, raising the question about who would follow Jaber as emir. On the Jaber side was Sabah Ahmad, brother, close advisor of the emir, and foreign minister.

Jaber quickly decided for Saad after a family council in which Jaber Ali's supporters walked out in anger. Jaber Ali did remain in the Council, however, as information minister. Key positions were given to the Jaber branch. Only the most powerful ministries were retained by the Sabah family, but that was enough to keep control.

This shifting of power between the two branches with the emir's branch gaining the best positions has caused a number of tensions in the past. As Kuwait has changed over the years, the ruling family has been able to retain power. With threats from powerful neighboring countries and with domestic tensions, these rulers may have difficult years ahead.

gible to vote from thirty to twenty years. In 1996, only 107,000 of Kuwait's two million residents were registered voters. Hundreds of women held demonstrations at polling places on election day to demand a higher degree of political freedom and the women's right to vote.

Candidates for the Assembly must possess the right to vote, be

The sweeping roofs of the National Assembly building, designed by Danish architect Jorn Utzon, evoke Bedouin tents.

over the age of thirty, and be literate. In the 1992 election, there were 278 candidates. Those not of the Sabah party took thirty-one of the fifty seats. Some nineteen seats were thought to be held by conservatives. The 1996 election saw a reduction in seats held by the religious fundamentalists. While political parties are not allowed, a number of organizations represented in the Assembly reflect various interests: Islamic Constitutional Movement (Sunni Muslim and moderate), Kuwait Democratic Forum (secular and liberal), Salafeen (Sunni Muslim and fundamentalist), National Islamic Coalition (Shiite Muslim), and Constitutional Group (merchants).

The Assembly meets for at least eight months a year. New elections are held within two months after the legislature is dissolved. The Assembly may vote a lack of confidence in a minister, requiring the minister to resign. While it does not have this power with the prime minister, it can approach the emir about the resignation of the prime minister. Then the emir must dismiss either the prime minister or the Assembly.

The emir may ask the Assembly to reconsider proposed legislation he does not like. If the Assembly still passes it by a two-thirds majority at its next session, then it becomes law. The emir may declare martial law (emergency powers) but only with the approval of the Assembly.

Kuwaitis are guaranteed a number of public liberties. Although prepublication censorship of the press has been lifted, punishment for harming the nation is possible. Moreover, the

Opposite: **Members of the National Assembly**

A Kuwaiti news broadcaster. The state controls all broadcast media in Kuwait.

state controls the broadcast media. Although Kuwait ratified the 1979 United Nations convention promoting equal treatment of women in 1994, it excepted from approval voting rights for women and equal standing in child custody issues. Still, in comparison with some of its even more restrictive neighbors, Kuwait has come a long way in recognizing political rights since the Persian Gulf War. It has the most progressive constitution among the Gulf states.

A unified judicial system was adopted in 1960. Before then, Islamic court applied Islamic law. Now there are six kinds of courts handling different types of cases: Constitutional Court, Court of Cassation (verdicts from Court of Appeal and the State Security Court), Court of Appeal, Court of First Instance, Summary Court (in each province with one or more divisions), and Traffic Court.

After the Gulf War, a Martial Law Tribunal dealt with the cases of persons accused of collaborating with the Iraqis. In 1993, the court gave a life sentence to a Kuwaiti for killing a Lebanese father and son whom he believed collaborated with Iraq. In 1994, after the assassination plot against U.S. President George Bush, a three-judge panel conducted a year-long trial. They sentenced five Iraqis and one Kuwaiti to death by hanging and seven others to six months to twelve years. One was found not guilty. Human rights groups complained that torture was being used to get confessions.

Because abuse of migrant domestic workers has been a problem in many Gulf states, a 1995 decision drew news comment when a court sentenced a Kuwaiti woman to ten years in prison for beating her maid to death.

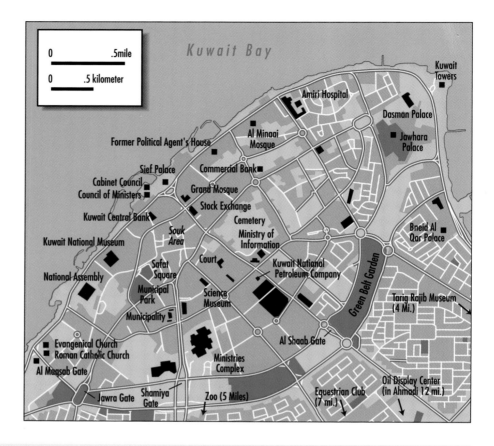

Kuwait Bay

0   .5mile

0   .5 kilometer

Kuwait Towers

Amiri Hospital

Dasman Palace

Al Minaai Mosque

Jawhara Palace

Former Political Agent's House

Sief Palace

Commercial Bank

Cabinet Council
Council of Ministers

Grand Mosque

Kuwait Central Bank

Stock Exchange

Cemetery
Ministry of Information

Bneid Al Qar Palace

Kuwait National Museum

Souk Area

Court

Kuwait National Petroleum Company

National Assembly

Safat Square

Green Belt Garden

Municipal Park

Science Museum

Tariq Rajib Museum (4 Mi.)

Municipality

Al Shaab Gate

Evangenical Church
Roman Catholic Church

Ministries Complex

Al Maqsab Gate

Jawra Gate

Shamiya Gate

Zoo (5 Miles)

Equestrian Club (7 mi.)

Oil Display Center (in Ahmadi 12 mi.)

Kuwait City: Did You Know This?

Kuwait City was built on a piece of land jutting into the natural harbor known as Kuwait Bay. Just outside of the bay in the Persian Gulf is the island of Faylakah, the home of Kuwait's most ancient ruins. These can be visited today, although the island was heavily mined by the Iraqis during the Persian Gulf War. In the past, the natural harbor provided Kuwaitis a rich living in fishing and pearl diving. Dependence on the sea, however, ended after the 1930s when oil was discovered in Kuwait. Today, the sea supports Kuwait in a different way. Enormous oil tankers carry oil from Kuwait to ports around the world.

The name Kuwait is a diminutive form of "kut," an Arabic word for fort. The earliest inhabitants of Kuwait City built a fort on Kuwait Bay and the settlement eventually grew into Kuwait City.

Kuwait City is the home of most of Kuwait's minority populations, along with the oil refineries. After the Persian Gulf War, however, when the Palestinians sided with Iraq, many were expelled. Many foreign nationals work in the country. The population of non-Kuwaitis may actually exceed the population of Kuwaitis.

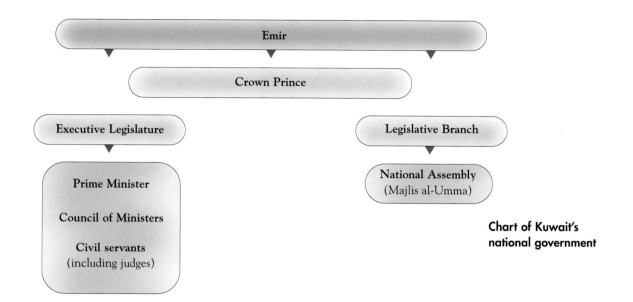

```
Emir
  │
Crown Prince
  │
  ├──────────────────────────┐
Executive Legislature    Legislative Branch
  │                          │
Prime Minister           National Assembly
                         (Majlis al-Umma)
Council of Ministers

Civil servants
(including judges)
```

Chart of Kuwait's national government

Kuwait City's Telecom building

There are five governates or provinces: al-Ahmadi, Farwaniya, Hawalli, al-Jahra, and Kuwait. The capital of the nation is Kuwait City.

Defense

In 1995, Kuwait had an active armed forces of 16,600: 10,000 in the army, 2,500 in the air force, 2,500 in the navy, and 1,600 foreign personnel. The national guard totals 5,000. The budget for the ministry of defense is 20 percent of the total budget. In addition, there are 1,111 United Nations unarmed troops and observers. The United States has moved troops to Kuwait as needed to counter Saddam Hussein's threats.

Two years of compulsory military service is required. University students have to serve only one year.

Primary school is free in Kuwait.

These girls are in secondary school.

Education

Kuwait has a free system of kindergarten, primary, intermediate, and secondary school. Compulsory education for children between the ages of six and fourteen was started in 1966. Some children, however, will start kindergarten two years before and go on to complete their education at eighteen. Private schools exist for those who prefer them.

A student will have primary education for four years followed by four years of intermediate education. The optional secondary education is another four years, usually in general schools. Specialized training is available in commercial, technological, health, and religious institutes. Eleven institutes are available for handicapped children.

The teacher-training college, technical college, and a university had some 20,000 students in the early 1990s. In addition, about 4,500 Kuwaiti students received education abroad. In 1996, the Assembly voted to segregate male and female classes in colleges and vocational schools. Classes were already separate in state-run secondary schools.

The literacy rate in Kuwait has been very high for the Middle East. Efforts to combat illiteracy and provide adult education have meant that some 60,000 men and women graduated from learning centers between 1969 and 1985.

Social Welfare Programs

With the help of money from the oil sales, Kuwait established a far-reaching social welfare system. Public assistance was given to widows, orphans, the disabled and sick, and low-income families.

Medical treatment was free until 1984 when a policy of the patient's paying 40 percent of the cost was put into effect. The country has modern hospitals that are well-staffed. For the 1995–96 financial year, the central government allocated 6.7 percent of the budget for public health.

Kuwait, Inc., has before it the difficult job of rebuilding a country that it did so much to modernize in the first place. Physical scars have been easier to remedy than the emotional ones. The rebuilding effort has used up some of the money that Kuwait had set aside as a reserve for when the oil supplies are used up. How Kuwait manages its economy will be of great importance to the future survival of the nation.

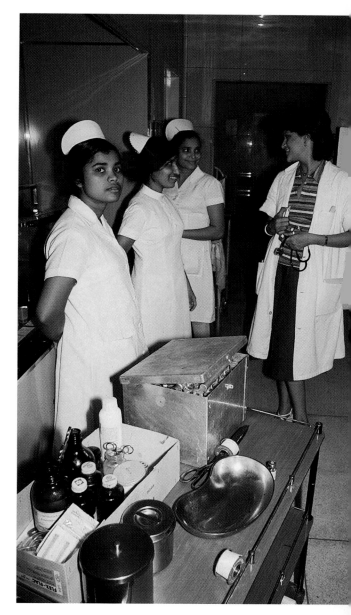

Kuwait has modern hospitals and well-trained staffs.

Oil and Money

Suppose you had been appointed chief economic advisor to the emir of Kuwait. The emir might ask you how he could best use the current wealth of his country.

Opening pearl oysters

Y OU WOULD HAVE TO TAKE INTO account the resources of the country. You would realize that you did not have much to work with beyond the oil and natural gas. These products once used are not replaceable. The value of pearl fishing, for which Kuwait was famous in history, has been hurt by the development of cultured pearls— pearls grown like crops rather than hunted by risky diving. Shipping ventures might be worth investigating—not in dhows (the sailing ships) but in big tankers and freighters. The waters around Kuwait present a hazard because they are bordered by enemies such as Iraq and Iran.

So you have a nation that has power now because of the petroleum products that are so vital to the interests of the industrialized Western nations. That power and wealth has attracted the interest of your enemies. The wealth has made Kuwaiti citizens hungry for many luxury products. Yet the oil reserves are going to run out in time, or perhaps a new source of power will be discovered that will mean that oil is no longer so valuable.

You will probably advise the emir to continue to set aside large money reserves from the oil products to provide a cushion for when the money is not coming in from an expendable natural

Kuwait citizens enjoy their wealth.

resource. The advantage of these cash reserves is that they can be invested anywhere in the world. You can diversify your investment—spread out risk and benefit over a larger geographical area, over many industries, and over many corporations. You may even win friends for Kuwait by investing money in countries that need funds.

Kuwait has invested large amounts of money in these reserves. Now the reserves themselves cause your enemies to envy you. Moreover, you have to invest these reserves well, or they might be lost. However, you have developed a new resource now and a cushion for the future.

What Kuwait Grows, Manufactures, and Mines

Agriculture

Tomatoes	35,000	metric tons
Cucumbers and gherkins	17,000	metric tons
Onions	16,000	metric tons

Manufacturing

Cement	533,000	metric tons
Ammonia (urea)	300,000	metric tons
Flour	127,000	units

Mining

Sulfur	175,000	metric tons
Lime	35,000	cubic meters

Petroleum and Natural Gas

Petroleum and its derivatives (the products that can be made from it) accounted for 93.8 percent of Kuwait's export revenue in 1994. This industry, however, employs a relatively small part of the population.

In 1990, before the Iraqi invasion, Kuwait had proven recoverable reserves of petroleum of 94,500 million barrels that at 1989 production levels would not be exhausted for 162 years. Even taking into account the Iraqi torching of some of these reserves, Kuwait had 96,500 million barrels in 1995 representing 9.6 percent of the world's reserves. Also, Kuwait has important reserves of natural gas associated with the petroleum deposits.

In spite of the damage the Iraqis did to the refineries, pipelines, and equipment, Kuwait has the capacity to produce 2.5 million barrels per day. This exceeds the 1.5-million-barrel level before the Iraqi crisis and the 2.0-million-barrel level that is the production quota agreed upon by the oil exporting countries.

The quick recovery has been surprising. The capping of the burning oil fields involved teams from many nations working under very difficult and dangerous conditions. Yet the job was done in record time. To produce revenue while the petroleum industry was being rebuilt, Kuwait asked the other Gulf States in the six-nation Gulf Cooperation Council to produce petroleum on its behalf. With the help of others and with the resources in its reserve fund, Kuwait has been able to surpass its precrisis levels of production in the oil industry.

Money

The second most important source of revenue is investment abroad. It was estimated that in 1993, Kuwait had between $35 billion and $45 billion invested in the United States, western Europe, and Japan. It had sizable amounts in all the New York Stock Exchange's top 100 corporations.

Many investments of this type were held by the Reserve Fund for Future Generations (RFFG). By law, 10 percent of petroleum revenues must be put in this fund to provide an income in the future. Prior to the Iraqi invasion, this fund was thought to have amounted to some $100 billion. By early 1996, the amount in this fund had fallen to an estimated $35 billion.

The Kuwaiti cost of the military operation for liberation in 1990–1991 was about $22 billion. Rebuilding costs amounted to about $20 billion. About half the RFFG investments were sold and $5.5 billion was borrowed from others to cover these costs. It has been estimated that the total losses from the Iraqi invasion and occupation amount to some $170 billion.

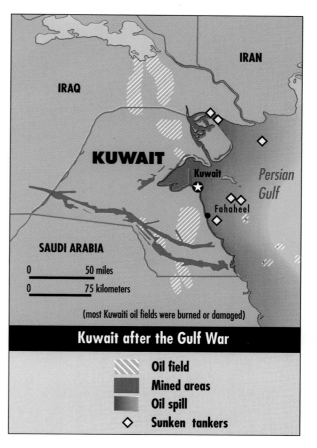

(most Kuwaiti oil fields were burned or damaged)

Kuwait after the Gulf War

Oil field
Mined areas
Oil spill
◇ Sunken tankers

The privatization or sale of some previously government-run industries has brought in some money. The government, however, has felt it necessary to spend on weapons and military training. With the government operating at a budget deficit, the government plans to reform the welfare system and cease some of its subsidies to public services. It has proposed increasing revenue by raising customs fees and imposing a direct tax on industrial and commercial profits.

Opposite: **Drilling for oil**

Other Industries

In the decade between 1974 and 1984, the manufacturing segment of the economy grew at an annual rate of 6.48 percent. After that, manufacturing was still increasing but at a much slower rate. The government wanted to diversify the types of industries in the country so that there would be other alternatives to petroleum.

Three industrial zones were set up at Shuaiba, Shuwaikh, and Ahmadi. Some of the new

Opposite: **The stock exchange in Kuwait City**

The main financial street in Kuwait City

Money Facts

The Kuwaiti dinar (KD) has 1,000 fils. There are coins of 1, 5, 10, 20, 50, and 100 fils, and notes of 250 and 500 fils and of 1, 5, 10, and 20 Kuwaiti dinars. In 1997, the exchange rate was 1KD=$3.3661 (or 1U.S.$=KD 0.2971)

Currency and Coins During Wartime

The symbols on the Kuwaiti currency and coins are similar to those on the Kuwaiti emblem. A nation occupied as Kuwait was in 1990–1991 faces special problems with its currency. The Iraqis forced the Kuwaitis in the occupied territory to turn in their Kuwaiti money and use Iraqi money. When the Iraqis withdrew their armed forces, the Kuwaitis had the problem of what to do about the Iraqi currency and the Kuwaiti money.

Less than a month after liberation, on March 24, 1991, the Kuwaiti government introduced a new currency. This tactic was a way to keep control of the economy so that Iraq could not counterfeit Kuwaiti money as easily. However, the country faced the problem of how to convert the old money into the new currency.

industries introduced include fertilizer, salt, and chlorine manufacturing.

Kuwait has not been enthusiastic about planning heavy industrial projects at home because of the demand for excessive foreign labor. However, it has entered into joint projects with other Gulf countries for plants elsewhere.

Some factories supply consumer goods such as foods, processed soft drinks, and flour milling. The construction industry was important even before the Iraqi invasion. The country built roads, bridges, houses—even entire towns. Kuwait had a building materials industry and related projects such as aluminum extrusion.

The government has favored Kuwaiti firms—and, since liberation, also corporations of the nations of the coalition forces—in assigning contracts. It has given protection to certain local industries, such as underwriting local costs so that the consumer would not have to pay higher prices because of tariffs on foreign goods.

As Kuwait's economy grew, so did the nation's need for electrical power. Water demands also increased. Kuwait has been using its petroleum and natural gas together with imports of gas to generate electricity. The country has been experimenting with alternative power sources such as solar energy in the desalination of water (eliminating the salt). The government has subsidized most of the actual electricity costs.

Most of the increased need of the Kuwaitis for water has been met through desalination. Underground fresh water supplies, however, have been tapped as has brackish water that is blended with distilled water and used for irrigation, watering livestock, construction, and in the household.

Opposite: **The trading floor of the stock exchange**

Oil and Money **87**

An aerial view of a desalination plant in Shuaiba, Kuwait

Harbors, roads, and airport construction before the Iraqi invasion had provided Kuwait with good facilities. The country relied on its road system rather than railroads. A good international airport serves Kuwait City. In 1990, the Kuwait Airways Corporation owned nineteen aircraft that flew to forty-one destinations. Iraq seized at least fifteen civilian airplanes but claimed that seven had been destroyed in coalition bombing in Iraq. The rest are to be returned.

Kuwait, known for its ship building and merchant fleets in history, still has a substantial merchant fleet of tankers and cargo vessels now being built elsewhere. During the Iran–Iraq war, Kuwaiti shipping was at risk.

Telephone lines and equipment is another industry that boomed with the country's economic growth. The use of cellular phones is said to have played an important role in the resistance efforts against the Iraqis.

Kuwait Airways is the country's primary airline.

Agriculture and Fisheries

Because of the lack of water and soil conditions, little grain is grown in Kuwait. The principal crops are tomatoes, cucumbers and gherkins, onions, melons, and dates. The country has been

These tomatoes are cultivated inside.

Kuwait has experienced growth in its numbers of livestock.

experimenting with new forms of agriculture such as hydroponics, which involves growing plants in solutions rather than soil.

Because the main source of food of the Bedouin historically has been herds of animals, the government encouraged animal husbandry. Poultry and dairy industries have been increasing in the private sector. Although there was growth in numbers of cattle sheep, goats, and poultry, Kuwait still imported considerable numbers of livestock and had investments in foreign agricultural companies.

During the Iraqi invasion, one herd of 2,155 imported cattle was destroyed, with only 182 in poor condition surviving. Some of the cattle were stolen by the army. Some died for lack of feed.

The effect of the burning oil wells on the remaining livestock raised health concerns. The numbers of livestock have increased since 1992.

Government plans for increasing the fishing industry received a setback from the oil spills. Local fisheries had been able to supply only 25 percent of the demand for fish even before the occupation. The catch of fish increased between 1992 and 1993 while the shrimps and prawns diminished. Over-fishing and long-term effects of the oil spill raise questions for this industry.

A fish farm

A Conversation between Kuwaitis and Friends from Canada and the United States

Ahmad: Kuwaitis should be the ones to benefit from our oil wealth. We have always taken care of our family, our tribe, our nation. Outsiders only lead to trouble.

Joe: My family immigrated to Canada, and now we consider ourselves Canadians. Sure, we benefited from the wealth of Canada, but now we are contributing to it. How are you Kuwaitis going to run the country alone?

Fatima: I think we women can do more. I would like to put my education to good use by working for my country, but my family does not like to have me work outside the home.

Jane: I hope your family will change. I would like to see you be able to use your talents the way I can in the United States.

System of Weights and Measures

The metric system is the legal standard in Kuwait, but some imperial weights and measures are also in use as are some U.S. measures.

Service Industry and Labor

Service industries employed 73.2 percent of the Kuwaiti labor force in 1988. One of the difficulties the Kuwaiti government faces is the large number of foreign nationals in the work force. According to estimates from a 1995 census, Kuwaiti nationals are only 41.6 percent of the population in Kuwait. Other Arabs, Iranians, Indians, and Pakistanis are the largest groups of non-Kuwaitis.

After the terrorist attacks that Kuwait has suffered and with outsiders coming to Kuwait to take advantage of its economic conditions, it is understandable that the government is sensitive to ensuring that Kuwaitis get good treatment. The problem of training Kuwaitis to do jobs they have not undertaken in the past and may not like to do in the future remains. Also, there is the difficulty of finding good labor to support economic growth.

Kuwaiti families enjoy
spending time together.

People of the Fort

If Kuwait means "fort," then the Kuwaitis can be considered "people of the fort." If fort seems a little old-fashioned, consider that the Kuwaitis are sitting on what is now a very valuable piece of oil-soaked real estate. During the twentieth century, they have been attacked by their three big neighbors, Saudi Arabia, Iraq, and Iran. Their occupation by the Iraqis triggered "Desert Storm." They now have some of the most modern weapons—stealth fighters—in their defense.

OUTSIDERS THINK OF KUWAITIS IN MANY DIFFERENT WAYS. They are the wily resistance fighters who were subjected to the worst that the Iraqis could devise, who suffered immense hardships, and who fought bravely for their country. They are the newly rich kids who are spoiled and pampered, who cannot do any dirty work, and who act like spoiled brats when they vacation outside their country. They are the smart merchants who have parlayed the luck of living on top of oil into an investment empire that makes their poor relatives envious.

Kuwaitis enjoy a relaxing afternoon.

Who Are the Kuwaitis?

The Kuwaitis are Arabs who honor both their Bedouin and seafaring merchant traditions. They have a love of the desert even though they have moved into the city. They may still raise camels and enjoy a picnic in the desert when they can do so in an area without the hazard of mines. They also are skillful merchants who used to take their sail-powered dhows to trade in faraway lands and who now trade stock and real estate in distant nations. Instead of diving for pearls, they now drill for oil to make money.

People of the Fort   **95**

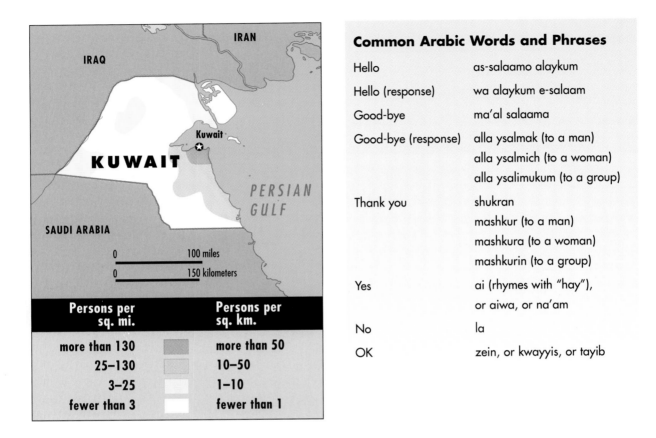

Common Arabic Words and Phrases

Hello	as-salaamo alaykum
Hello (response)	wa alaykum e-salaam
Good-bye	ma'al salaama
Good-bye (response)	alla ysalmak (to a man)
	alla ysalmich (to a woman)
	alla ysalimukum (to a group)
Thank you	shukran
	mashkur (to a man)
	mashkura (to a woman)
	mashkurin (to a group)
Yes	ai (rhymes with "hay"),
	or aiwa, or na'am
No	la
OK	zein, or kwayyis, or tayib

The founding families came from the Anaiza tribe of a powerful federation of north Arabian tribes, the Adnani, who can trace their ancestors back to pre-Islamic times. Their language is Arabic although English is widely understood.

Arabic is spoken in many countries from North Africa to the Mediterranean and the Gulf. There are many dialects. A Moroccan may not understand a Kuwaiti though both are speaking versions of Arabic.

Arabic is a sacred language because it is believed that the Koran, the sacred book of Islam, was transmitted in Arabic. The

Opposite, top:
A modern shopping mall

language also has been used for great litera-ture. Poetry is especially valued, and the language with long and short syllables is well adapted for this literary form.

Written Arabic can be very beautiful and has been made into an art form by the Muslims. The Classical Arabic is the lan-guage of the Koran. It is the form from which all other versions have come. A modernized and simplified form is called Modern Standard Arabic. It is used in newspapers and the media. Also, it is employed by the educated classes especially when an Arab is communicating with someone from another part of the Middle East. There is a still more simplified form that can be used in a script form.

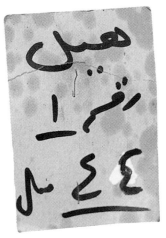

The Arabic language can be written in elaborate or sim-ple forms.

What about the Foreigners Living in Kuwait?

With the discovery of oil, people came flocking to Kuwait in search of the new jobs created by the new industry and the new wealth. The population went from an estimate of 152,000 in 1950 to 2,048,422 by mid-1989. The highest growth rate recorded for any independent country was chalked up by Kuwait between 1963 and 1970 when the average annual increase amounted to 10 percent.

As of 1995, the estimated population was 1,697,301. The Iraqi crisis of 1990–1991 and its aftermath sent many foreign nationals scurrying. Even before then in answer to the security issues posed

Arabic Numbers

0	sifir
1	wahid
2	ithneen
3	thalatha
4	arba'a
5	khamsa
6	sitta
7	sab'a
8	thimania
9	tis'a
10	ashra
11	hda'ash
12	thna'ash

An Iranian immigrant selling goods at the market

by terrorists, the government had adopted the policy of Kuwaitization—doing without nonessential foreign labor when possible. In April 1995, from preliminary census results, Kuwaiti nationals still accounted for only about 41.6 percent of the population.

Before the oil boom, foreign elements were present in the population of this nation of traders. Africans were an important minority. Powerful Arab families brought slaves from Africa. Slavery is no longer legal. Descendants of the slaves, however, may remain as family servants.

The Persians from Iran constitute another minority. These people often retained their language and belonged to the Shiite branch of Islam. They kept to themselves, rarely intermarrying with the Arabs.

The Indian community tended to be shopkeepers, tailors, cleaners, or domestics. Some of them were brought in by British families during the period of strong British influence in Kuwait and India.

With the conflict in Palestine at the time of the establishment of Israel, many Palestinians fled to Kuwait to set up homes and raise their children. After the Iraqi occupation with which some Palestinians sympathized, this element of the population was under suspicion.

The increasing wealth of Kuwait attracted from other countries many Arabs who had professional and technical training.

Largest Cities in Kuwait	
Salimiyah	130,215
Jaleeb ash-Shuyukh	102,178
Hawalli	82,238
South Kheetan	63,628
Farwaniya	53,100
Sabahiya	50,535
Kuwait City	28,859

Egyptian workers looking for employment in Kuwait

Many Kuwaitis hold top positions, such as these engineers.

Palestinians and Egyptians played important roles in the fields of medicine and education. Syrians and Lebanese were prominent in business and trade. Many other nationalities were represented in the unskilled labor force.

Because of the wealth that has come to many Kuwaitis, they do not need to work with their hands. If they do enter the workforce, they are given priority in promotions and receive special treatment.

Because foreign nationals have a twenty-year wait to become citizens and because most foreign workers can come to Kuwait for only limited periods of time, this group of people presents a problem for Kuwait. They lack political privileges and may resent the opportunities of the Kuwaitis. Especially in the unskilled jobs, the high turnover makes for a less-than-efficient workforce.

Who Lives in Kuwait?

Kuwaitis 41.6%
Other nationalities, including
Arabs and non-Arabs 58.4%

A trader on the stock exchange

Islam—The Straight Path

Almost all of the people living in Kuwait are Muslims (believers in Islam). Most of these are Sunnis, the largest branch of Islam. Around 30 percent are Shiites, the next largest branch. There are Christian churches in Kuwait: the Roman Catholic Church (Latin, Melkite, and Syrian rites), the Anglican Communion (Episcopal), and the National Evangelical Church. Foreign workers have brought their Hindu and Buddhist faiths with them.

U NDER THE CONSTITUTION, PEOPLE ARE GUARANTEED THE freedom of performing religious rites according to prevailing customs provided these do not violate public order and morality. In 1996, there was concern over a Kuwaiti court's treatment of a Christian convert from Islam. That person found it necessary to come to the United States. Subsequently, he returned to Kuwait, his family, and Islam.

Children begin reading the Koran at an early age.

What Is Islam?

Islam is based on the revelations given to Muhammad beginning around A.D. 610 when he lived in Mecca in what is now Saudi Arabia on the Arabian Peninsula. He began receiving these revelations when he was about forty years old. He was to become the great prophet of Islam.

What did Muhammad expect of his followers? Islam means submission. Allah is the Arabic word for God. Muhammad called on people to submit to Allah. In the first revelation recorded in the Koran, he asked to be shown the "straight path."

The five pillars of Islam are duties that Muslims are expected to perform as part of their obligation toward God. The *Shahadah*

Muhammad (c. A.D. 570 to 632)

Muhammad's father died before his son was born. He left his son only a small inheritance—five camels, some sheep, and a slave girl named Baraka from Abyssinia in Africa. Muhammad grew up poor, not liked by his rich relatives.

Because his mother was sick and thought her son could be better cared for away from unhealthy Mecca, she sent him to a hill town, Taif, in the care of a shepherd and his wife. When he was about five, Muhammad had the first of his visions and frightened the family with whom he was living. He was returned to his mother, who died shortly thereafter leaving Muhammad an orphan with only Baraka as a possession.

It was Baraka who led him to the house of Abd al-Muttalib, a kindly man, who taught Muhammad about the worship of the moon god. Abd al-Muttalib died two years later. Muhammad went to live with his uncle, who had the child work as a shepherd. When he was about ten, his uncle let him accompany one of the caravans going north as a camelman and guard. This was the beginning of many caravan trips during which Muhammad often talked with priests and rabbis when he was stopped at trading posts. Muhammad could not read or write, but he possessed a fine memory and later recalled details of his journeys. However, he had no prospects for becoming wealthy or a leader.

When he was about twenty-five, Khadija, a rich widow of about forty, heard that Muhammad was a good camel driver and caravan manager. She took a liking to Muhammad and married him. They had six children, two boys who died in infancy and four girls. Every night he worshiped at the Kaaba, a great black stone associated with the religion of the goddesses of power, fate, and fertility as well as other idols.

An artist's depiction of Muhammad, upon whose revelations Islam is based

Religions of Kuwait

Islam is the state religion and 90 percent of the population is Muslim. Sixty-three percent of the Muslims are Sunni and 27 percent are Shiite. Other religions such as Roman Catholicism and Anglicanism are represented but mostly by the foreign communities working in Kuwait.

After the first revelation when he was about forty, he rushed back to Khadija, who reassured him that he had been visited by angels and not devils. This revelation and others that were to follow were collected in the Koran. When he began to preach against idol worship, he was almost strangled before he was rescued. For many years he was detested by the people of Mecca.

After a plot to murder him, Muhammad and his followers made their escape from Mecca and went to Yathrib, a city to the north, where they had been invited to come. Yathrib was later renamed Medina. The year was 622. This flight from Mecca to Medina was a turning point for Islam and is known as the hegira, which means "breaking the bonds." This event became the beginning date of the Islamic calendar. At Medina, Muhammad established his rule, and Islam began to spread. He fought with the people of Mecca. Eventually that city fell without a fight in 630.

Muhammad fleeing to Medina

Muhammad lived only two more years but was active in planning the spread of Islam. He had many wives after the death of Khadija. Ayesha was one of the most famous.

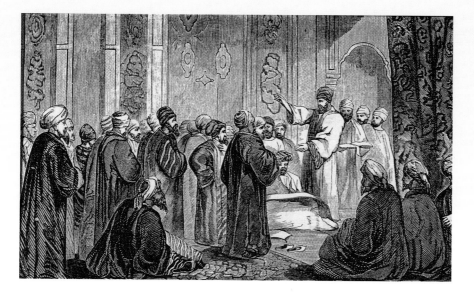

Followers of Islam listening to Muhammad speak

is a confession of faith that the Muslim must declare as belief: "There is no God but the one God, and Muhammad is His prophet." Of course, there is more to Islamic beliefs—Paradise, angels, the Last Day. It is the Shahadah, however, that is repeated many times during the day.

Salat, or the ritual prayer, is required five times a day, at dawn, noon, late afternoon, sunset, and after sunset. The believer prepares by a ritual washing—water, if available, but sand will do where there is no water. The prayer begins in a standing position and follows with bows and prostration where the forehead touches the ground. Quotations from the Koran or other sources are repeated silently.

Zakat is the giving of alms to the needy. It is based on a formula depending on the kinds of property owned by the believer. In addition, voluntary contributions above what is required are seen as a way of gaining merit.

The prostration of ritual prayer

Sawm is the fast during the month of Ramadan—a month that depends on a lunar calendar so it changes throughout the secular year. The fast is for the entire day, from daybreak until sundown. Food, drink, and smoking are forbidden during this period. The family will share a meal before dawn and after sunset. When the month of Ramadan falls during the long and hot days of summer, the fasting can be a test of self-control. There are exceptions to this requirement for travelers, the sick, and some women.

A family enjoying a meal together after a fast

Finally, the *hajj*, or pilgrimage to Mecca, is expected of Muslims once during their lifetime, if they have the money to pay for the trip. Some make the trip repeatedly, but for others it is the climax of years of preparation. The ceremonies in Mecca take several days and involve going around the Kaaba, kissing the black stone in one of its corners, and sacrificing a sheep.

A view of ancient Mecca

Varieties of Muslims

The two major branches of Islam—Sunni and Shiite—came into existence at the very beginning of Islamic history. The two had different ideas

Mosques and Minarets

A Muslim does not have to pray in a mosque (above), the building set aside for congregational prayers, but the practice is encouraged. On Fridays, there is a service in the mosque for prayers and a sermon from the leader, who is sometimes called the imam.

The designs on a mosque may be very beautiful, but you will not find pictures that could be worshiped as idols. Often verses of the Koran in very beautiful script decorate the interiors. In addition to the stairs to the place from which the sermon is preached, there will be a niche that marks the direction of Mecca to which the believers turn when they pray.

A minaret (below) is a high tower from which comes the call to prayer. Traditionally, a man called the muezzin climbed up the tower to call the faithful to prayer five times a day. Now, you are more likely to hear a recording of the call.

The Grand Mosque in Kuwait City was opened in 1986 at a cost of KD 13 million. The building can accommodate 5,500 persons.

about how the successor to Muhammad should be chosen. Also, there are differences in their interpretation of the law and in their practices and heroes.

These two are not the only branches to be found in the Arabian peninsula. Through the years, differences in emphasis have caused new groups to form. Also, there are different interpretations of Islamic law that once controlled the entire life of Muslims. Now, most Muslim countries have adopted modern law codes so that traditional laws apply mainly to personal cases involving family and inheritance. In addition to this emphasis on law, there is a strong tradition of mysticism in groups such as the Sufis.

In many Islamic countries at the present time, there is a tug of war between people who favor traditional ways (often called fundamentalists) and those who want to see more modern practices that are in harmony with Islam. In Kuwait, these conflicts have been reflected in different views of the role of women. Since the Gulf War, some women have achieved important positions in government and education, but they still cannot vote.

Religious Holidays Determined by Lunar Calendar

Muslim New Year
Laylat al-Miraj
Milad an-Nabi
'Id al-Fitr
'Id al 'Adha

Muhammad taught that Jews and Christians should be accorded somewhat higher status among other religions as "People of the Book" who acknowledge one God and with whom Muslims share some prophets. Muslims believe that there may have been as many as 240,000 prophets and recognize Moses, Abraham, Joseph, David, and Jesus as prophets. However, they acknowledge Muhammad as the "Seal of the Prophets." Muhammad was the last of the prophets because the revelation of the Koran was all that was needed. Persons converting from Islam may find themselves disowned by their families and under death threats. Theoretically the practice of religion is protected by the state under the constitution as long as the acts do not violate public order or morality.

Opposite: **A mosque adjacent to a modern high-rise**

Kuwaiti Culture

Kuwaitis are very proud of their heritage. They have collected some of the finest examples of Islamic art. They have preserved the poetry, dances, and customs of their ancestors. They are also tough competitors at sports.

ISLAM, THE BEDOUIN CULTURE, THE MERCHANT TRADITION, and the Iraqi occupation are important influences on Kuwaiti life today. In Islamic culture, because representing life forms that can be worshiped is forbidden, beautiful art forms have developed. The Koran forbids the use of alcohol. Kuwaitis influenced by Western customs interpret this restriction broadly, especially when out of the country. Four wives are permitted in Islam if the husband can treat all of them equally.

An example of Bedouin weaving

From Bedouin life comes the strong loyalty to tribe that translates to the extended family and to the nation. Hospitality is a keynote for desert life, where survival may well depend on receiving food and water from a stranger. Fierce fighting was encouraged by the frequent raids of one tribe against another for their livestock. One's honor is a person's most valuable possession.

The Kuwaiti merchant is known as a wily trader who can bargain well. Those who sailed their ships to faraway countries had to be willing to take risks. Wealth is valued for the power it brings.

The recent events of the Iraqi occupation have left their mark. Kuwaitis still fear Iraq and have not been repaid for the destruction that the Iraqis brought to their homes and cultural institutions. Among the first collaborators tried in 1991 were seven actors, poets, and songwriters who were given life sentences and four musicians and artists who were given five to fifteen years in prison. The Kuwaiti lawyers have prepared an extensive war-crimes case against Saddam Hussein and 115 Iraqis for their brutal treatment of Kuwaitis. Iraqi music is banned.

The Arts

Traditional decorative art is highly prized. The Islamic books such as the Koran have beautiful calligraphy (a decorative script). Many Islamic books were hand copied and decorated in rich colors. Bedouin weaving is another art form that has found markets worldwide. The ability to make elaborate jewelry, the wealth of a woman in the past, continues to be a valued craft.

Kuwaiti jewelry for sale in a shop

Today, Kuwait encourages modern artists. From the 1950s, the schools have been teaching art. A National Council for Culture, Arts, and Letters was founded in 1974 and has encouraged Kuwaiti writers and artists. It sponsors an annual competition of children's paintings.

With the building boom, architecture has become important. The skyline of Kuwait City is punctuated by the three concrete towers that house the city's water supply, two restaurants, and a good vantage point to see the Gulf. These were opened in 1979 but were closed after the occupation because of the damage caused by the Iraqis.

The typical Kuwaiti home has several rooms for entertaining. Often the men and the women have separate rooms for greeting friends. Because of the wealth from the oil industry, many Kuwaiti houses are very elegant. Before the widespread introduction of air conditioners, wind towers called barjeel were used to cool houses. The towers, open on all four sides, catch any breezes and pull them down a central shaft to the room below.

One of the most interesting places to visit is the old covered souk or marketplace. Here you will find gold sellers and electronics shops, money changers, and meat markets. Merchants of one product tend to group together. Some of the areas of the souk were badly damaged in 1991, but others are in good condition.

The souk, or marketplace

Music and dances are a valued part of Kuwaiti heritage. Drums, tambourines, and a kind of animal-skin bagpipe are some of the usual musical instruments. The men dance the Ardah with

Painting and Sculpture

In 1936 when Kuwait granted scholarships in the arts to its students, it was the first country of the Gulf states to do so. The nation can boast the most advanced modern art movement in the area.

The first painter from the Gulf region to depict local subjects was Mojab Dossari (1921–1956). He trained abroad in Egypt. Most of the Kuwaiti artists have concentrated on realistic subjects such as landscapes, portraits, or still life.

However, a few have chosen the symbolic subjects of surrealism. Sami Muhammad (born in 1943) is a painter and sculptor of that school. He trained in Cairo and the United States. His most famous monument in Safat Square represents an open oyster with a pearl inside the shell.

A Kuwaiti artist sells her work in a square.

swords. The women have traditional wedding dances. Some old songs are those the sailors sang while out on the pearling ships.

Poetry has always been an important Arabic art form and way of passing along tribal history. Today, movies and theater performances are available. TV, radio, newspapers, and magazines supply the news.

Museums

The respect of the Kuwaitis for their heritage and their future is seen in the number of museums they have built. The showcase for the ruling family's fine collection of some 7,000 pieces of art and 8,000 coins was the National Museum. The Sheikha Hussah al-Salem al-Sabah, together with her husband, Sheik Nasser Sabah al-Ahmed al-Sabah, had loaned to the National Museum their superb collection of Islamic art. It was a comprehensive collection from all parts of the Muslim world and throughout several periods of history. The museum also contained items from the Faylakah Island archaeological excavations and a display featuring the Bedouin culture.

During the early period of the Iraqi occupation in 1990, someone familiar with the National Museum reported seeing four large Iraqi army trucks parked at the museum and heard soldiers remov-

Tareq Rajab Museum

The Tareq Rajab Museum is in the basement of a large home. After you enter, on your left is a display of Arabic manuscripts and calligraphy. In this hall you will see examples of ceramics and pottery from various Islamic countries. (In many mosques, tiles of many colors and designs cover the exterior and the inside of the buildings.)

On the right of the entrance you find a display of traditional costumes and jewelry. Included here are costumes not only of the Arab Middle East but also from Asiatic countries such as Kazakhstan and Uzbekistan.

The National Museum

ing cases from the building. Taking fragile manuscripts and wooden architectural features from their air-conditioned home and transporting them across the desert could have damaged the works of art. To prevent the items from being sold on the art market, Sheikha Hussah sent detailed descriptions of the items in her collection to international organizations in Paris. Fortunately, at the time of the invasion more than one hundred items from the collection were on loan to international museums in Russia and the United States.

When the Iraqis left, they smashed what remained and set fires to the areas in which the al-Sabah collection and the archaeological finds were housed. They also torched the Planetarium, which was part of the museum.

The outside of the museum looks all right, but enter the building, and you will see melted metal handrails and galleries that

A monument to the Iraqi invasion

A Kuwaiti Wedding

Because Kuwaitis are in many ways the most sophisticated of Gulf people, they may not follow all the customs of a traditional Arab wedding. Today, with young people frequently traveling abroad and influenced by other ideas, they may be more ready to choose their own spouses and customs, such as the white bridal dress.

Because of the importance of the family in Arab culture, marriage and the selection of the right partner is crucial. In traditional families, mothers may scout around to determine the best prospects. Nevertheless, it is the prospective bridegroom's father who, with his son, approaches the bride's future father to discuss a match. The potential bride's father asks for a few days in which to give his answer. If he does not already know all about the son, he will make inquiries and will consult his daughter.

If the match is agreed upon, then the two families set a wedding date. The marriage contract is made in the presence of a representative of the Islamic faith. The money the bridegroom gives to the bride is not the purchase of the bride but a gift that she may spend as she likes. Divorce is fairly easy for the man, except that he has to give his wife a large sum of money. She then returns to her father's home.

The night before the wedding, the women gather at the bride's home for a party. They may paint the bride's hands and feet with fancy designs in red henna (below), a powder made from the dried berries of a bush. The women may dance the Muradaa in two rows going forward and back while chanting the praises of the bride.

Not to be outdone, the men dance the Rizeef in two lines facing each other. With the beat of the drum and tambourine, they stamp back and forward chanting the praise of their tribe. The men may carry a rifle or a bamboo cane. They may shoot off their rifles in celebration. Bands with traditional instruments provide music.

When the bridegroom takes his wife to his home, he has full responsibility for her support.

A day at the zoo

Kuwaitis enjoy boating and other water sports.

have been turned to ash. The Kuwaitis have decided to leave this part of the building as a memorial to what the Iraqis did. A hall at the back of the museum was prepared to receive what little the Iraqis returned.

The Science and Natural History Museum has a collection of taxidermic animals (stuffed and mounted), some animal skeletons including those of several dinosaurs, and a space exhibit. The Iraqis destroyed items in the transportation exhibit.

In addition to national museums, a number of private citizens had their own collections of Islamic and Kuwaiti art. One of the museums that survived the Iraqis and is open to the public is the Tareq Rajab Museum, which houses the collection of the first minister of antiquities.

Also, Kuwait has two zoos, a small archaeological exhibit on Faylakah Island, and an Oil Display Centre that contains exhibits about the petroleum industry at al-Ahmadi.

Sports and Entertainment

With the wealth that many Kuwaitis enjoy, they have time for sports of many kinds. Before the occupation, when mines planted on the beaches (as well as those that washed ashore) were not a problem, water sports such as windsurfing, waterskiing, scuba diving, and yachting were big attractions. Because jellyfish are out for most of the year, swimming pools have been built even on public beaches.

Among the spectator sports are cricket, rugby, and soccer. Because the Kuwaiti team has had some international success, soccer is probably the most popular.

The Touristic Enterprises Company runs government projects such as sea clubs, recreational parks, beaches, an ice skating rink, a musical fountain, a yacht club, a swimming pool complex, the Kuwait towers, and an entertainment center.

Liberation Tower

Daily Life for Ahmad and Fatima

Ahmad and Fatima, who lived through the Iraqi occupation, are now young adults. They are more serious than their Kuwaiti friends who were abroad at that time. They put their lives on the line for their country. They want to live in a free Kuwait and see their nation prosper.

Both Ahmad and Fatima have attended schools in classes where boys and girls were separate. They both have plans for further education abroad. Ahmad, in addition to attending his regular classes, has gone to an Islamic school to study the Koran.

122

BOTH PLAN TO BECOME PROFESSIONALS—AHMAD AS an engineer in the oil industry and Fatima as a physician. Their family is able to provide the support for a comfortable lifestyle. The government provides its citizens with social benefits and welfare, thereby spreading the oil wealth to even Kuwait's disadvantaged citizens.

Rosa has returned home, but other servants from foreign countries have taken her place. Neither Ahmad nor Fatima would want to do the jobs of the servants. No Kuwaitis wanted this work.

Ahmad and Fatima have talked about the possible future problems their country could have with their big neighbors. How can they ever feel safe when Kuwait's oil and wealth have attracted such unwelcome attention as the Iraqi occupation? Both Ahmad and Fatima have suffered nightmares and flashback memories of what they saw during the occupation.

Still, there is little that they can do now except go on with their daily life. What is that life like?

A Kuwaiti Day

The first call to prayer at dawn wakes Ahmad and Fatima. They say the first of their five prayers and then gather in the cool morning air for a light breakfast with their family. Of course, during Ramadan, the month of fasting, a meal before dawn is

Many Kuwaiti dishes include seafood, such as this Gulf shrimp salad.

This three-day holiday marks the end of Ramadan. It is a time of rejoicing and visiting friends. Traditionally, a lamb or goat is killed and cooked. The meat is piled on a huge serving plate heaped with rice and dates. Coffee is served along with a very sweet desert made of crushed sesame seeds and honey.

Official Kuwaiti Holidays

New Years' Day
January 1

Emir's Accession Day
February 25

Kuwaitis wear both Western-style and traditional clothing.

necessary since the fast cannot be broken until the sun goes down. Other holidays, such as the Eid al-Fatr, involve feasting.

Meals are generally taken with the family. If the parents are entertaining, then the children may eat beforehand. Because of the many cultures living in Kuwait, food of many nationalities may be found from fancy French dishes, to Indian curries, and American hamburgers. Fish and food with spices are common. Dates are a favorite.

For recreation after school, Ahmad is likely to enjoy a game of soccer with his friends. Even young boys will practice kicking and blocking a soccer ball. Fatima is more likely to go with her friends to the souk to see what is on sale and to talk with others.

Clothing

Both Ahmad and Fatima are dressed in western-style clothing for school although both have beautiful traditional robes in their wardrobes for ceremonial occasions. In Kuwait, it is unusual for women to wear the long black robe and veil that is common in other parts of the Arab world. However, some of the young women who have been swayed by the Fundamentalists have begun wearing the traditional garments again. Fatima feels that a lady should dress modestly—but that is all that the Koran requires of a woman.

The traditional dress of an Arab woman is a long gown with gold or silver embroidery at the neck, sleeves, and hem. A long black cloak and veil cover this garment when the woman goes out in the street. For parties, colorful, spangled gowns of silks and satins may be worn. Now wealthy Kuwaiti women are likely to have fine clothing from the latest foreign designers.

Traditionally, the men wore long robes of cotton for summer and wool for winter. A large scarf is placed on the head and kept in place with a black rope. The rope was originally used to hobble camels in the desert so they would not wander too far. During the Iraqi occupation, the Kuwaitis joked that the leaders the Iraqis claimed were Kuwaitis did not even know how to wear this scarf in the traditional Kuwaiti manner with a dip in the front. For dress occasions, the men will wear lightweight brown or black cloaks edged with gold.

Men often wear scarves, secured by black ropes, over their heads.

Soccer—A Favorite Game

Soccer, known in most of the world as football, is a sport that many Kuwaitis enjoy as players and spectators. It is a team game of skill and strategy. There are many techniques of kicking and blocking the ball. Because the field is large and the game is fast-paced, it requires stamina and strength to play.

Daily Life for Ahmad and Fatima **125**

Kuwaitis enjoy very strong coffee.

When entertaining, the men and women will often gather separately in different rooms called *majlis* or *diwaniyya*. Incense will be burning in a container, often made of brass or silver with fancy decorations.

Very strong coffee is served while the people talk. The coffee cups are kept filled until the guest shakes the cup slightly from side to side to indicate that no more is wanted. Then servants will bring the incense burner and a flask of rosewater around. The rosewater is poured into the hands of the guests, who will put it on their face and hair. Then the one with the incense container will approach the guests so that the fragrance can be inhaled. This ritual is a sign that the party is over, and the guests depart.

Coffee—A Gift from an Arabian Goat

Thanks to a frisky goat, the benefits and joys of coffee were discovered. According to this story, a shepherd in one of the Red Sea Arabian countries—most likely Yemen—noticed that his goat jumped around more after he nibbled on coffee plants. The shepherd decided that the plant might be a good way to stay awake. One of the uses of coffee was discovered.

The beverage took Europe by storm. At one time coffeehouses were the center of social life. There are many kinds of coffee. The Arabic variety is served in small cups and is very, very strong.

The Future

What can Ahmad and Fatima expect for the future? As long as oil is as important to the Western industrialized nations, they can count on significant military assistance in countering the enemies of Kuwait.

When oil runs out or when another source of fuel supplants oil, then Kuwait is banking on its accumulation of wealth to give the Kuwaitis an opportunity to continue the current lifestyle. Yet will foreigners be made uneasy by the Kuwaiti investments in their countries?

Within Kuwait, there are tensions. Will the rulers be able to provide a high enough standard of living to keep the not-so-wealthy citizens and poor foreigners content? Will the more conservative Muslims and the more liberal Muslims find a way to live together? How much democracy will the country permit? As Kuwaitis travel and live abroad, will they continue to be satisfied with their form of government? Or will they react against the excesses they see in other countries and become even more traditional?

A modern apartment building

Ahmed and Fatima cannot know the future of their country. The better they educate themselves, the better they will be able to serve Kuwait.

Timeline

Kuwaiti History

Earliest known civilization exists in Kuwait.	**2200** B.C.
Kuwait is a principal link on major trade route.	**500** B.C.
Kuwait under the rule of the ancient Greeks	**4th century** B.C. to A.D. **1st century**
Hijira (migration) of Muhammad from Mecca to Medina; start of the Islamic era	**622**
Muslims conquer Syria, Iraq, and Kuwait.	**633–637**
The Portuguese occupy the Persian Gulf.	**1507–1650**
Several clans from the Anaiza migrate from the Arabian Desert to Kuwait.	**1716**
The first ruler of Kuwait, Sheik Sabah 'Abd ar-Rahim, is chosen.	**1756**

World History

2500 B.C.	Egyptians build the Pyramids and Sphinx in Giza.
563 B.C.	Buddha is born in India.
313	The Roman emperor Constantine recognizes Christianity.
610	The prophet Muhammad begins preaching a new religion called Islam.
1054	The Eastern (Orthodox) and Western (Roman) Churches break apart.
1066	William the Conqueror defeats the English in the Battle of Hastings.
1095	Pope Urban II proclaims the First Crusade.
1215	King John seals the Magna Carta.
1300s	The Renaissance begins in Italy.
1347	The Black Death sweeps through Europe.
1453	Ottoman Turks capture Constantinople, conquering the Byzantine Empire.
1492	Columbus arrives in North America.
1500s	The Reformation leads to the birth of Protestantism.
1776	The Declaration of Independence is signed.

Kuwaiti History

British war ships clear the Persian Gulf.	**1860**
Sheik Mubarak as-Sabah invites British protection from the Ottoman Empire.	**1899**
Kuwait's borders are demarcated but not ratified in a treaty between Great Britain and the Ottoman Empire.	**1913**
British troops defend Kuwait against incursions from the Ottoman Empire.	**1914–1918**
The Conference of Uqair attempts to negotiate boundaries between Kuwait, Iraq, and Saudi Arabia.	**1922**
Oil production stops.	**1939–1945**
Kuwait becomes a fully independent state.	**1961**
Kuwait adopts a constitutional monarchy.	**1962**
Kuwait joins the United Nations.	**1963**
Kuwait, Saudi Arabia, the United Arab Emirates, Qatar, Oman, and Bahrain found the Gulf Co-operation Council (GCC), a security organization.	**1981**
Iranian attacks on Persian Gulf shipping prompt Kuwait to request U.S. protection for Gulf shipping.	**1987**
Iraq invades Kuwait; the Persian Gulf War starts.	**1990**
U.S.-led international coalition drives Iraqi forces from Kuwait, ending the Persian Gulf War.	**1991**
Saddam Hussein again claims that Kuwait is an Iraqi province.	**1992**
U.N. Security Council reaffirms the border between Kuwait and Iraq.	**1993**
Iraq recognizes Kuwait as a sovereign nation and agrees on boundaries.	**1994**

World History

1789	The French Revolution begins.
1865	The American Civil War ends.
1914	World War I breaks out.
1917	The Bolshevik Revolution brings Communism to Russia.
1929	Worldwide economic depression begins.
1939	World War II begins, following the German invasion of Poland.
1957	The Vietnam War starts.
1989	The Berlin Wall is torn down, as Communism crumbles in Eastern Europe.
1996	Bill Clinton is reelected U.S. president.

Fast Facts

These towers dominate the Kuwait City skyline.

Official name: State of Kuwait (Dawlat al-Kuwayt)

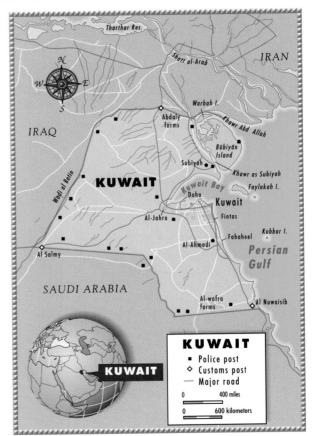

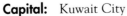

Capital: Kuwait City

Official language: Arabic; the Arabic spoken in Kuwait is closer to classical Arabic than many of the dialects spoken in the Middle East.

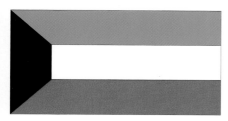

Flag of Kuwait

Official religion: Islam

National anthem: National Anthem (melody only, no words)

Government: Constitutional monarchy with one legislative body (National Assembly)

Area: 6,880 square miles (17,818 sq km), including the Kuwaiti share of the Neutral or Partitioned Zone

Bordering countries: Saudia Arabia, 101 miles (163 km); Iraq, 160 miles (257 km); Persian Gulf shoreline, 132 miles (212 km)

Head of state and government: Emir

Total boundary length: 598 miles (963 km)

Highest elevation: A 900-foot (275-m) prominence in the southwest corner of the country and a 400-foot (120-m) ridge at Mina' al-Ahmadi provide the only breaks in Kuwait's stretches of desert and mud flats.

Lowest elevation: Sea level at the coastline

Average temperatures: Summer temperatures range from 84°F (29°C) in the morning to 125°F (52°C) at midday; during the night in the winter temperatures occasionally reach the freezing point.

Average annual rainfall: 4 inches (10 cm)

National population: (1995 est.) 1,697,301

Population (1995 est.) of largest cities in Kuwait:

Salimayah	130,215
Jaleeb ash-Shuyukh	102,178
Hawalli	82,238
South Kheetan	63,628
Farwaniya	53,100
Sabahiya	50,535
Kuwait City	28,859

Shopping at the souk

Famous landmarks: The Red Fort (Al-Jahra); National Museum (Kuwait City); Tareq Rajab Museum (with a fine collection of Islamic art, is located in Kuwait City); Sief Palace (Kuwait City); the Sadu House of Bedouin arts and crafts (Kuwait City); Kuwait Towers (Kuwait City)

Industry: The discovery of oil in Kuwait radically changed the economy of the country. Oil is now the main-stay of the economy and provides the Kuwaitis with one of the highest standards of living in the Middle East. Oil is responsible for 45 percent of the Gross National Product (GNP) and 90 percent of export earnings. Aside from oil Kuwait has reserves of natural gas and produces cement and fertilizer from its mineral deposits. Small manufacturing plants, however, produce ammonia, fertilizer, paper products, processed foods, and other consumer goods. Farming contributed less than 1 percent of the non-oil GNP of Kuwait before the Persian Gulf War. Nevertheless, the government subsidizes agri-culture, and the primary crops are vegetables, melons, and fruits.

Currency: The Kuwaiti dinar (KD) has 1,000 fils. There are coins of 1, 5, 10, 20, 50, and 100 fils, and notes of 250 and 500 fils and of 1, 5, 10, and 20 Kuwaiti dinars. 1997 exchange rate 1 KD=$3.3661 (or U.S.$1=KD 0.2971)

Weights and measures: Metric system

Literacy: 79.7%

Mosques have beautiful architectural lines.

Common Arab words and phrases:

shamal	a cool summer breeze
tauz	a fierce dust storm that hits Kuwait in winter
emir	an Arab chieftain and the official name of the ruler of Kuwait since 1962
sharia	the code of law prescribed by Islam
as-salaamo alaykum	hello
wa alaykum	response to hello
ma'al salaama	good-bye
alla ysalmak	response to *ma'al salaama* (if speaking to a man)
alla ysalmich	response to *ma'al salaama* (if speaking to a woman)
alla ysalimukum	response to *ma'al salaama* (if speaking to a group)
shukran	thank you
mashkur	thank you (to a man)
mashkura	thank you (to a woman)
mashkurin	thank you (to a group)
ai (rhymes with "hay"), or *aiwa*, or *na'am*	yes
la	no
zein, or *kwayyi*, or *tayib*	O.K.

To Find Out More

Nonfiction

▶ Bratsman, Fred. *War in the Persian Gulf*. Brookfield, CT: The Millbrook Press, 1991.

▶ Dutton, Roderic. *An Arab Family*. Minneapolis: Lerner Publications, 1985.

▶ Foster, Leila M. *The Persian Gulf War*. Chicago: Childrens Press, 1991.

▶ Foster, Leila M. *Saudi Arabia*. Chicago: Childrens Press, 1993.

▶ Fox, Mary Virginia. *Iran*. Chicago: Childrens Press, 1991.

▶ Fox, Mary Virginia. *Bahrain*. Chicago: Childrens Press, 1992.

▶ Fakhro, Bahia, and Walko, Ann. *Customs of the Arabian Gulf*. Hamden, CT: Arab Customs, 1978.

▶ Hoad, Al, and Abdul Latif. *Islam*. New York: Bookwright Press, 1987.

▶ Kent, Zachary. *The Persian Gulf War: "The Mother of All Battles."* Springfield, NJ: Enslow Publishers, 1994.

▶ Nardo, Don. *The Persian Gulf War*. San Diego: Lucent Books, 1991.

Fiction

▶ Matthews, Mary. *Magid Fasts for Ramadan*. New York: Clarion Books, 1996.

Reference

▶ David, Peter. *Triumph in the Desert*. New York: Random House, 1991.

▶ Editors of *Time*. *Desert Storm*. New York: Time Warner, 1991.

▶ Hawley, T. M. *Against the Fires of Hell: The Environmental Disaster of the Gulf War*. New York: Harcourt Brace Jovanovich, 1992.

- Powell, Colin. *My American Journey*. New York: Random House, 1995.

- Schwarzkopf, H. Norman. *It Doesn't Take a Hero*. New York: Bantam, 1992.

Videotapes

- Heller, Joel, with Dan Rather. *Desert Triumph*. New York: CBS News, 1991.

Websites

- **Arabnet—Kuwait**
  http://www.arab.net/kuwait/kuwait_contents.html
  A full range of cultural, geographical, and tourist information on Kuwait

- **City.net—Kuwait**
  http://www.city.net/countries/kuwait/
  Links to many Kuwait-related web pages

- **Tareq Rajab Museum**
  http://www.kuwait.net/~trm/index.html
  A virtual tour of this privately owned Kuwaiti museum

Organizations and Embassies

- Embassy of Kuwait
  2940 Tilden Street, NW
  Washington, D.C. 20008
  (202) 966-0702

- **Radio Kuwait**
  http://www.radiokuwait.org/
  Listen to RealAudio broadcasts from Kuwait

- **Embassy of Kuwait**
  http://www.EmbassyOfKuwait.com/main_index.html
  Travel, geographical, cultural information from the Kuwaiti Embassy in Canada

Index

Page numbers in *italics* indicate illustrations

Meet the Author

HOW DO YOU TELL THE EXCITING STORY OF WHAT HAPPENED TO Kuwait during Desert Storm? I collected newspaper and magazine articles about that period. Then I began imagining what it would be like to have lived through Desert Shield and Desert Storm inside Kuwait. Ahmad, Fatima, and their family and friends are fictional characters, but I tried to make their lives as true to the accounts that I read as possible.

Kuwait has a distinguished history long before the 1990s. I had to dig in books to learn about that history and to discover how the nation managed its government and economy. Other books and magazines helped me to understand better that nation's religion and culture. One of Kuwait's most remarkable achievements has been its recovery from the Iraqi occupation. For that I had to follow the daily news sources—from newspapers to web sites.

Someday I would like to visit Kuwait. I have traveled in Iraq, Iran, Yemen, Egypt, Syria, Israel, Jordan, and Lebanon in days when such trips were possible. Travel and photography are two of my hobbies.